Literature & Thought

WIDE OPEN SPACES

AMERICAN FRONTIERS

Perfection Learning

EDITORIAL DIRECTOR   Julie A. Schumacher

SENIOR EDITORS   Rebecca Christian, Terry Ofner

EDITORS   Rebecca Burke, Sherrie Voss Matthews

PERMISSIONS   Lucy Anello, Adam Conley

RESEARCH ASSISTANT   Suzanne Foggia

REVIEWERS   Laurie Bauer

Leone Jungk

DESIGN AND PHOTO RESEARCH   William Seabright and Associates,
Glencoe, Illinois

COVER ART   WILD HORSES OF NEVADA 1927 Maynard Dixon

ACKNOWLEDGMENTS

"The Captives" by Stephen Vincent Benet from *The Last Circle*, Farrar, Straus & Company,
copyright 1946 by Rosemary Carr Benet. Copyright renewed 1974 by Thomas C. Benet, Rachel Benet Lewis and
Stephanie B. Mahin. Reprinted by permission of Brandt & Brandt Literary Agents, Inc.
     "The Courtship" by George Ella Lyon from *The Music of What Happens*, edited by Paul B.
Janeczko, copyright © 1988. Reprinted by permission of the author.
     "End of the Trail" by Jim Kjelgaard from *Buckskin Brigade*, copyright © 1945. Reprinted by
permission of the author.
     "First Encounter" from *The Journal of Christopher Columbus* by Cecil Jane, translator.
Copyright © 1960 by Clarkson N. Potter, Inc. Reprinted by permission of Clarkson
Potter/Publishers, a division of Random House, Inc.
     "A Friend of the Indians" by Joseph Bruchac from *Wounds Beneath the Flesh*, edited by Maurice Kenny,
copyright © 1987. Reprinted by permission of the author.
     "Gold Rush!" composed of "Gold Mine Found," from the *Californian*, reprinted courtesy of
the Bancroft Library, University of California, Berkeley, and "The Gold Fever," from *The Hartford Courant*, Copyright
The Hartford Courant, reprinted with permission.
     "Levi's," a letter from Jacob W. Davis to Levi Strauss & Co., July 2, 1872, as reprinted in Ed Cray, *Levi's*
(Boston: Houghton Mifflin, 1978). CONTINUED ON PAGE 144

WHAT IS THE LURE OF THE FRONTIER?

The question above is the *essential question* that you will consider as you read this book. The literature, activities, and organization of the book will lead you to think critically about this question and to develop a deeper understanding of the frontier.

To help you shape your answer to the broad essential question, you will read and respond to four sections, or clusters. Each cluster addresses a specific question and thinking skill.

CLUSTER ONE What were explorers seeking? **ANALYZE**

CLUSTER TWO What were the effects of Manifest Destiny?
COMPARE AND CONTARST

CLUSTER THREE Who were the people of the frontier? **SUMMARIZE**

CLUSTER FOUR Thinking on your own **SYNTHESIZE**

Notice that the final cluster asks you to think independently about your answer to the essential question — *What is the lure of the frontier?*

WHERE THE DESERT MEETS
THE MOUNTAIN
Walter Ufer

Where West Is

Long before we were born
the people who lived in the world
had their way of finding west
without the use of delicate instruments.

One of them whose duty it was
to find west would begin to walk
in the direction of the setting sun
while chanting the tale of the world
in his head.

When he was finished
he would bend down and
draw a line in the dirt
with his finger.

Beyond this line
everything was west.

Thom Tammaro

WIDE OPEN SPACES

AMERICAN FRONTIERS

TABLE OF CONTENTS

CLUSTER THREE   Who Were the People of the Frontier?

Thinking Skill SUMMARIZING

CLUSTER FOUR THINKING ON YOUR OWN

Thinking Skill SYNTHESIZING

The Lure of the Frontier

 sk a deep-sea diver why he explores the ocean floor or an astronaut why she wants to be the first settler on Mars. The answer may well be "Because it's there."

From earliest times the frontier has lured adventurers to forsake the comforts of home for a plunge into the unknown. Explorers in America set out seeking everything from land and gold to an escape from the long arm of the law. The nobler sought liberty. Some merely yearned for a new place to call home. Whatever the quest, the frontier has always begun at the border of the known and unknown.

That's why the frontier keeps moving. Once the Atlantic seaboard—now the "old" part of the United States—was itself a frontier. For the Pilgrims, it was a wild new world. By the time the colonies declared independence from Britain in 1776 the Atlantic seaboard had become tamed. After winning the Revolutionary War, Americans began the relentless push west that helped give them the can-do spirit and national identity that still exists today.

INDIANS FLEE IN FEAR
OF COLUMBUS
1495
Giuliano Dati

Algonquian Indian
conjurer

FUR TRADERS DESCENDING
THE MISSOURI
1845
George Caleb Bingham

ESSAY 9

THE TRAIL OF TEARS
1942
Robert Lindneux

By horseback, foot, covered wagon, and train, the settlers moved from the wooded mountains of the East to the open, treeless plains of the Midwest. Here the wind moaned through the tall grasses and the horizon could suddenly turn black with herds of buffalo. The change from the citified East was so drastic that some settlers went mad.

As Europeans moved in, some tribes were destroyed by diseases brought by early settlers; others were forced to abandon their traditional way of life as they were "civilized" and made to adopt European languages and religions. Later, tribes such as the Cherokee were forcibly moved from their homes in the East to the dry, parched land of Indian Territory, now the state of Oklahoma.

Yet the pioneers pressed on. Westward expansion was so rapid and thorough that by 1820, all lands east of the Mississippi were inhabited. The next wave of adventurers crossed the swiftly flowing waters of that mighty river. They continued into the desolate Great Plains and beyond to the Big Sky Country of the true West. And when gold was found in California in 1848, adventurers rushed pell-mell to the Pacific Coast.

Conestoga wagons
pulled by oxen
transported
pioneers across
the plains.

10   ESSAY

In 1862, the Homestead Act lured still more settlers west with the promise of free land. Following the Civil War, expansion continued as the far western frontier was slowly turned into farmland. After the Oklahoma land rush of 1889, some observers worried that the frontier that had helped define the American spirit was gone.

They could not have imagined the moment in 1957 when the Russians launched the satellite Sputnik. Suddenly, Americans were faced with the vast new frontier of space. Twelve years later, it was an eerily magical moment for the entire world when American astronaut Neil Armstrong set foot on the moon. Since then other frontiers have opened. With the help of technology, medical experts have turned inward, finding new frontiers within the human body and searching for the keys to some of its most well-kept secrets. The very ocean that the Pilgrims crossed has, itself, become the focus for discovery. And cyberspace is often called the Wild West of high technology.

No, the frontier has not disappeared from American culture. As long as land, space, and science exist, so does the urge to explore it. Why? Because it's there.

Above: The coming of the railroad plus the greed of white hunters soon put an end to the massive herds of buffalo that roamed the plains.

Middle: Members of the Joseph Dehm family outside their Nebraska sod home

Below: A collage of lunar landscape photos. Space is one of man's newest frontiers.

CONCEPT VOCABULARY

You will find the following terms and definitions useful as you read and discuss the selections in this book.

49ers short for 1849ers; nickname for those who participated in the California Gold Rush which began in 1849

Boomers a nickname for people who rushed in to settle a new area

Conestoga wagon a covered wagon drawn by horses or oxen

frontier a region that is on the border of a settled and developed country; the limits of knowledge about a particular subject

frontiersman one who lives or works on the edge of a settled area

gap an opening or passage through a mountain range that allows for easier travel

Homestead Act of 1862 a law that allowed farmers to claim up to 160 acres of land free if they paid a small registration fee, lived on the land, and cultivated it for five years

homesteader one who acquires land by farming and maintaining property bought or deeded from the U.S. Government

Indians/Native Americans the indigenous peoples of North and South America

Manifest Destiny the belief that the United States had a God-given right to settle the entire American continent

mission any one of the churches built by Spanish Franciscan and Jesuit priests to educate, convert, and care for Native Americans

mountain man a person at home in the wilderness, such as a fur trapper

pioneer one of the first to settle in a new territory

ranchero Spanish for "rancher"

rugged individualism a strong belief in one's own ability to overcome any obstacle

soddy a home made from strips of sod stacked on top of each other

Sooner a person moving into an area before it is officially opened for settlement; also a nickname for Oklahomans

tenderfoot an inexperienced newcomer in a rough or newly settled area

trail boss the person in charge of a wagon train or a cattle drive

trailblazer one who marks a path for others to follow

treaty a contract signed between two governments or their representatives

CLUSTER ONE

What Were Explorers Seeking?

Thinking Skill   ANALYZING

Christopher Columbus landing on Hispaniola, 1492

First Encounter

Christopher Columbus

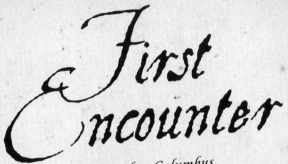

Christopher Columbus sailed east from Spain during the fall of 1492 in hopes of finding a shorter trade route to Japan, referred to in Europe as "the Indies." Seventy days later Columbus landed on an uncharted island in the Caribbean Sea. His exact landing site is unknown, but scholars believe it might have been the Bahamian island of San Salvador. In his diary, Columbus writes about the first sights and impressions this "new world" made upon him.

Thursday, October 11th

... *I*mmediately they saw naked people, and the admiral¹ went ashore in the armed boat, and Martin Alonso Pinzón and Vicente Yañez, his brother, who was captain of the Niña. The admiral brought out the royal standard, and the captains went with two banners of the Green Cross, which the admiral flew on all the ships as a flag, with an F and a Y, and over each letter their crown, one being on one side of the † and the other on the other. When they had landed, they saw very green trees and much water and fruit of various kinds. The admiral called the two captains and the others who had landed, and Rodrigo de Escobedo, secretary of the whole fleet, and Rodrigo Sanchez de Segovia, and said that they should bear witness and testimony how he, before them all, took possession of the island, as in fact he did, for the King and Queen,² his Sovereigns, making the declarations which are required, as is contained more at length in the testimonies which were there made in writing. Soon many people of the island gathered there. What follows are the actual words of the admiral, in his book of his first voyage and discovery of these Indies.

1 **the admiral:** Columbus was the admiral. He refers to himself in third person throughout his diaries.
2 **the King and Queen:** Ferdinand and Isabella of Spain

"I," he says, "in order that they might feel great amity towards us, because I knew that they were a people to be delivered and converted to our holy faith rather by love than by force, gave to some among them some red caps and some glass beads, which they hung round their necks, and many other things of little value. At this they were greatly pleased and became so entirely our friends that it was a wonder to see. Afterwards they came swimming to the ships' boats, where we were, and brought us parrots and cotton thread in balls, and spears and many other things, and we exchanged for them other things, such as small glass beads and hawks' bells, which we gave to them. In fact, they took all and gave all, such as they had, with good will, but it seemed to me that they were a people very deficient in everything. They all go naked as their mothers bore them, and the women also, although I saw only one very young girl. And all those whom I did see were youths, so that I did not see one who was over thirty years of age; they were very well built, with very handsome bodies and very good faces. Their hair is coarse almost like the hairs of a horse's tail and short; they wear their hair down over their eyebrows, except for a few strands behind, which they wear long and never cut. Some of them are painted black, and they are the colour of the people of the Canaries,³ neither black nor white, and some of them are painted white and some red and some in any colour that they

---

3 **Canaries:** a group of islands off the western coast of
Africa in the Atlantic Ocean

find. Some of them paint their faces, some their whole bodies, some only the eyes, and some only the nose. They do not bear arms or know them, for I showed to them swords and they took them by the blade and cut themselves through ignorance. They have no iron. Their spears are certain reeds, without iron, and some of these have a fish tooth at the end, while others are pointed in various ways. They are all generally fairly tall, good looking and well proportioned. I saw some who bore marks of wounds on their bodies, and I made signs to them to ask how this came about, and they indicated to me that people came from other islands, which are near, and wished to capture them, and they defended themselves. And I believed and still believe that they come here from the mainland to take them for

slaves. They should be good servants and of quick intelligence, since I see that they very soon say all that is said to them, and I believe that they would easily be made Christians, for it appeared to me that they had no creed. Our Lord willing, at the time of my departure I will bring back six of them to Your Highnesses, that they may learn to talk. I saw no beast of any kind in this island, except parrots." All these are the words of the admiral. ☙

INDIAN MASSACRE OF 1862
John Stevens

THE CAPTIVES

Stephen Vincent Benét

It was good to have news of you, my dear Charles—you have no idea how eagerly we seize upon the mails from Britain, in this exile. Even a six-months-old scrap of gossip is chewed like a bone. I've no doubt the same is true of all foreign service, but here, in the colonies of America, you may take it for a fact. Indeed, sometimes I wonder whether it is truly the year of our Lord, 1764, or if I but doze and hibernate, as bears are said to, in the wilderness.

My own budget will not repay yours, I fear. I cannot tell you of Lord X's duel with Lord Y, recount the witty things said by Mr. B—at the coffee-house, or how the world took Viscount Z's elopement to Gretna Green with the heiress. You question me as regards the late campaign, and, certainly, I shall do my best to inform you. To one who has played his part—and a noble one—in such a victory as that of Minden,[1] our backwoods scufflings here must seem unworthy [to] a true son of Mars.[2] Nevertheless, there are certain details you will not find in the newsletters, and it is for these I crave your attention. To tell you the truth, this American campaign has unsettled my mind in a way I would not have believed possible, when we last spoke together. And the chief reason for that unsettlement has nothing to do with either strategy or tactics. Perhaps it is part of the vein of superstition that you have ever

---

1 **Minden:** a fierce battle near the town of Minden, Germany, where the English and the Germans defeated the French in 1759 during the Seven Years War
2 **Mars:** the Roman god of war

claimed, though pleasantly, was a part of my Scots heritage. Yet I think we see things as clearly at Auchairn[3] as you do in London, and perhaps with a deeper vision. Well, well, to my tale.

As you doubtless know, our difficulties at the outset of the business were grave enough—the war[4] having broken out so suddenly and with such unexpected violence over the whole American frontier. I believe it to be generally thought, in England, that a few thousand whooping and painted savages are little to tax the strategy of a British general—and this after Braddock![5]—but, I assure you, it is not the case. No doubt they would be easy enough to deal with on the plains of the Low Countries, but here, in these loathsome and scarcely penetrable woods, it is a different affair. You smile a little—you have seen the forests of Germany. But these are not woods, they are wilderness. The tree-boughs meet above, the underbrush has never known the axe. At night there is a darkness of darkness and small, crying sounds. I despair of showing you the difference, yet it exists, like a creature that has not been tamed.

I joined the regiment in the West Indies, just in time to get my first dose of fever and sail for the Pennsylvania Colony with the effects still upon me. My Highlanders[6] had been riddled by the disease—it was pitiful to see their plight. There were clansmen of mine in the regiment and they depended upon me, as men will—I fear ineffectually, for the most part. Indeed, I will confess to you that there was a moment when I did not see what use we might be in an active campaign, even granting that we reached the port of Philadelphia alive. But I did not know our new commander, Colonel Henry Bouquet.

A Swiss, a free sword[7] of the old adventurous stripe and a most sagacious soldier—he had served under Forbes in the previous campaign

---

3 **Auchairn:** the fictional name of a Scottish castle; it also refers to the title the narrator will hold when he returns to Scotland, i.e., Laird Auchairn

4 **the war:** refers to the French and Indian War (1754–1763)

5 **Braddock:** General Edward Braddock led English and American troops into battle near Fort Duquesne (or present-day Pittsburgh) on July 9, 1755. The troops met a force of Canadians and Indians who shot at them from behind trees and underbrush. Braddock kept his troops in an exposed area in neat lines, and they were massacred.

6 **Highlanders:** a name for Scots from the northern area of Scotland; also a regiment in England's army

7 **free sword:** a mercenary, or hired soldier

and, in truth, did most of that business, Forbes being an old man and ailing. He is a red-faced man and careful of his dress, but you see the look of true command in his eyes. My Highlanders grinned woodenly when they heard that he was to lead them. For myself, I was perturbed at first, when I saw the exercises he put us to—for leaping over logs and darting from tree to tree are not part of the ordinary exercise of a soldier. There were those who thought it an undignified proceeding—they should try to cut their way through the wilderness of Pennsylvania. I can only say that my own men took to it like ducks to water—it was the way of fighting that we used at Preston Pans,[8] if you will pardon the analogy.

Well, I will not rehearse the events of the war. We beat the savages soundly at Bushy Run—they had thought to catch us there as they caught poor Braddock, but did not, thanks to our commander. A small affair, for Europe, but, I may say, fiercely contested. It is incorrect to believe the savages will not stand fire—they charge with great dash and spirit. True, if you break them, they will run—so will any troops. You must fight them their own way, if you are to succeed—not by set volleys of musketry. L–d J–f–y A–h–st[9] may be of a different opinion. I may say, and with no ill will, that I would L–d J–f–y had been at Bushy Run.

Well, we relieved Fort Pitt and, next year, pushed on to the Muskingum—it is a wide, flowing river. Now that is what I wish to talk to you about—you will think me daft for doing so, yet it weighs upon my mind. It was the question of the captives. Again, I despair of making you understand.

wooden war club

8 **Preston Pans:** a battle during the Scottish Jacobite Uprising of 1745, where Highlanders led by Charles Edward Stuart defeated British forces

9 **L-d J-f-y A-h-st:** The writer is criticizing Lord Jeffrey Amherst, a British Army general.

They had been captives for years, through all the Indian country. There were stolen girls who had grown to womanhood, there were men who had barely escaped the stake and the fire, there were children who had forgotten the sound of English speech. When we got to the Muskingum, the Indians began to bring them in. You have doubtless seen prisoners exchanged. This was not like that.

It was the season we call St. Martin's summer—a part of the autumn when, for a week or two, the warmth and the light of summer return, before the snow. They call it Indian summer here, and it is a most beautiful time. More beautiful than in England, for the sky seems made of blue smoke and the trees turn bright red and gold. It is dauntingly beautiful, yet there is something fey[10] about it. You would not think that a wilderness could look so fair and so peaceful. And yet the gold is fairy gold, and might vanish at a touch.

Now had we been but invaders—and, indeed, there were times when I felt strange enough—all might have been according to rule. But with us were the Virginia and Pennsylvania riflemen—and, many of them, come for that thing alone. It was their own blood and their own kin they sought to recover, not ours. That makes a difference. I shall try to describe them to you. They wear linsey shirts and leather breeches, they are tall, strong men. They are not rich in possessions yet they do not look like hinds or yeomen. They carry their rifles lightly and they walk with a long, springing step. You would know the likeness—you, who have seen our poor, proud clansmen in the Highlands. But these are Germans, Irish, English—God knows what they are, yet all walk the same and carry their heads high. I could understand it, at Auchairn—after all, we are all of the same stock there, and we cleave to the chief. But they have no chief and yet they have the pride. There is no one man among them who does not feel himself a man and the equal of any. They are difficult to command—yet I have seen them drive the head of a nail with a bullet at fifty yards. To be sure, they are both rough and rustic—it is a rough life they lead. Yet, somehow, it is *their* county, rather than ours—I can put it no other way and yet I know you will smile and ask me what I mean.

I had speech with a number of them—they were laconic but humorous. They were not always respectful of the prowess of British arms, but

10 **fey:** fairy-like; otherworldly

they liked Bouquet. Most of all they were anxious for the captives—I shall tell you of that.

When the first eighteen were brought in by the Delawares, I felt very appropriate sentiments, I can tell you. A pitiful troop they seemed, clad in skins like the savages themselves and so burnt by the sun as hardly to be distinguished from them. It was shocking to me to see those of my own kind and race reduced to such a condition. I expected to see anguish and horror writ clear upon every face. And yet, when the thing was accomplished—and it was not till after a deal of ceremonious speech-making—I saw a young, tow-headed Virginia rifleman step up to one of the wild figures.

"Well, Henry," he said with a drawl—they slur their speech in a manner I cannot reproduce—"You've kind of filled out in the brisket. But you're looking peart, at that."

"Thanks, Tom," said the strange, wild figure, in the same cant, "I reckoned if they sent a war-party, you'd be with it. Obliged to you. Say, have you got any Christian tobacco? I've been smoking willow-bark all winter. Wasn't bad, excepting for that."

Then the two brothers beat each other upon the back, whooping and swearing strange oaths that I did not comprehend. A tall, painted savage watched them; it seemed to me, scornfully. After a moment the brother who had been a captive, turned.

"Oh, Tom," he said, indicating the savage, "this here's Little Bear. He's a friend of mine. His ma 'dopted me. Guess if she hadn't, they'd have burned me—they seemed to be fixing to. But him and the old lady stood up for me something handsome. Treated me right. Like you two to be acquainted."

"That so?" said the other brother. He raised his hand and made a sign—it was odd to see a white man do it with the dignity of a savage.

"What's their word for peace?" he said.

The other brother gave it and he repeated it. Not a muscle seemed to change in the savage's countenance but now he, too, made a sign and began to speak.

"He's saying you're my brother so he's your brother," said Henry. "But you ain't to believe all he says—I helped him out in a pinch once, but why wouldn't I?" His tone was precisely the tone of an anxious collegian, introducing some new-found friend. "Where's that tobacco of yours? We'd better have a smoke on it. Say, that's fine."

It was then I began to understand a little of what goes on in these wildernesses. The man, Henry, was younger than I, yet to him captivity and rescue were part of the normal lot of life. That would be comprehensible in a soldier, but he was not a soldier. At the end, there was a ceremonious leave-taking between himself and Little Bear. Yet, when I had speech with him later, he talked to me as cheerfully of killing Indians as a man might of knocking over a hare. There was no inconsistency to it—he could not imagine a life lived another way.

I shall not describe all that I saw—it would take a better pen than mine. I have seen a woman dressed in skins give a wild high cry and run to the husband who had thought her lost forever. I have seen a woman from the pack-trains go endlessly up and down through the throng of captives, muttering, "A little boy named Jamie Wilson. Has anybody seen a little boy named Jamie Wilson? He wore a blue cap and is about ten years old." I have seen memory and recognition come back into a child's eyes, when, at first, he strained away from the strange, white faces and would have gone back to his savage foster-kin. There were women who had red husbands and red children. They were delivered over to us faithfully, loaded with the poor gifts of the woods, yet, before we had reached Fort Pitt, there were some who had slipped away and back to the bark lodges. We did our best to retain them—indeed, we bound one or two, though I thought that wrong—but the forest had entered into their veins, and they would not stay. I shall tell you of one other woman and then my tale will have an end.

It was part of my duties to help make out a muster-roll of the rescued—and this is how I first saw her. She had come in with a group from the villages of the Shawnees, but, though with them, she was not of them—she always stood a little apart. That is how I shall always think of her—a little apart from the rest. A gray-eyed girl, slight but strong, with hair that the sun had bleached to a silvery-gold. She was dressed, like the others, in the gear of the savage and there was an old Indian woman with her who made much of her and howled when she was taken away. She was perfectly biddable and quiet, but none appeared to claim her from among our men and women. Well, there were others in that case, and yet, somehow, she was different. There are wild legends of women turned into deer. I could believe them, looking at her face.

When there was an opportunity, I questioned her, though the opportunity did not come till the evening. I then saw that she was younger than I had imagined—indeed, she could not have been more than sixteen. She answered my questions pleasantly and with dignity, though there was little she could tell. She had been captured, as I gathered, somewhere in Western Pennsylvania and she knew her name to be Mary. But of what her last name had been she had no recollection, though, she assured me, she had often tried to recall it. The cabin had been beside a stream, but to each name of a river that I mentioned she gravely shook her head. It was always called the river, to her remembrance—she could tell me no more.

No, she could not remember neighbors, but her father had worn a beard and her mother had had a red apron. There had been a little brother—she remembered the look of him very well. Then, one day, she had strayed into the woods, gotten lost, and fallen asleep. As she told it to me, gravely and sweetly, in her halting English, it was like one of our own old rude ballads of children stolen away to dwell in a green hill. For that was the last she saw of hearth and home. There were scalps at the belts of the raiding-party that found her—she thought one to be her mother's by the color and texture of the hair but she was not sure. This she told me with the unstudied, poignant matter-of-factness of a child. I gather, at the time, she must have been about six years old.

Why the Shawnees had spared her instead of despatching her I cannot tell—it is a thing that happens at times. Since then she had lived with them, not unhappily. From time to time she had seen other captives—so kept her English. There had been in particular, a woman named Margaret McMurtrie, a later captive and kind to her. She had tried to teach her something of white ways, though they did not always sound very comfortable. And now, after all this, she was going back to a white world.

It may not seem logical, but I cannot tell you how forcible an impression her recital made upon me. It was not only the story but the circumstances—the girl's clear, candid face in the red light of the campfire—the great sky above us with its stars. I wondered privately to myself why she, unlike so many others, had no Indian husband. Then, looking at her, suddenly I knew. There was a fey quality to her—an unawakened simplicity. I queried her.

"Yes," she said in her careful English, "they thought I helped with the corn. It is very important to have the corn good. They did not wish to give me a husband till they were sure the corn would like it. Perhaps they will take me back again, but I do not think so. You are very strong people, you English."

"I am Scots," I said, "not English. But you are English."

"Am I?" she said. "Well then, I suppose I am. But I do not know what I am." And she smiled at the fire.

"And what do you think of me—of us—now you have found us?" I said, with a man's blundering.

She looked me over gravely and candidly.

"Why, I think you wear very pretty clothes," said she, touching my sleeve with a child's inquisitiveness. "You must have wonderful animals to give you clothes like that."

That was how we talked together at first—and yet, how might I have done otherwise? I wish you would tell me. It was part of my duty to make out the rolls—part of my duty to assist the captives. The child could not remember ever having seen a wheeled vehicle before she came to our camp. Would you think I could play the schoolteacher? I would not have thought so myself. Yet I taught her the greater part of her letters, on our way to Fort Pitt and beyond it, and she proved an obedient scholar. You will say it is the Scotsman in me, yet you would have done the same. I could not bear to think of her as merely childish or a savage, when she looked at me out of her gray eyes. The Bible, fortunately, she knew of—her father had been wont to read a chapter of it aloud in the evenings, and that good woman, Margaret McMurtrie, had been a professing Christian. We used to read a chapter of it aloud, by the campfire, and I would expound it to her as best I might. Now and then I would hit upon some verse that touched a chord of memory and a puzzled, rapt expression would come upon her face.

You see it was my thought—God knows why—that if, by any means, I could make her remember her name and more of her past history than she knew, the spell of the wilderness might be shaken from her. I do not know why I thought so—and, indeed, it will seem to you a matter of little import. What matter if she lived and died, unlettered and savage? There are many such, in the wilderness. And yet, it mattered to me. I knew how a man must feel whose bride has been, as we say, fairy-kist, and comes back to him out of the green hill, but not as she went away. Yet I did my best—you will laugh to hear what I did. By the time we had passed Fort Pitt, she could say the first half of her catechism very fairly. Yet, if I must be honest, it did not seem to me that she spoke with understanding. She would repeat her answers as well as any lass, but I could not feel that grace had penetrated her heart. Yet it was not a hard heart, nor a recalcitrant,[11] as I should know.

The belief of the Indians is not easy to set down, yet, at the core, it is simple. They are not blind idolaters, like the pagans of old, and they worship a spirit or presence, though they name him differently. At least, that is what she told me. I should be glad to think she told me truly. It is hideous to think of whole nations consigned from birth to the pit or the flame, though John Calvin[12] makes no bones about it. Yet she must have been baptized a Christian, even if she could not remember it. I keep cleaving to that.

I remember one night when we were talking and she told me of the devils in tree and water that her friends also believed in. At least they seemed like devils to me, though perhaps they were not. I could not bear to hear her and I groaned aloud.

"Why, what is the matter? Are you sick?" she said, with her candid stare at me and the light on her silver-gold hair.

"No, not sick," I said.

"If you are sick," she said, "why, that's easy, for a man. You will go to the sweat-lodge and feel better. But, I forget—you English do not use the sweat-lodge."

"Child," I said, very gently, "will a time never come when you say 'we English' instead?"

"I try to say that," she said. "But I forget." It maddened me, for some reason, to hear her say so without fear or shame.

"Woman," I cried, like any dominie,[13] "have you no fear of God's judgments? Do you not see that every day you have spent in the wilderness has been a day without grace?"

---

11 **recalcitrant:** stubborn, defiant

12 **John Calvin:** a French religious reformer and theologian who believed people could be saved only by the grace of a Christian God

13 **dominie:** clergyman

"I do not know what you mean," she said. "Sometimes the sun shines and sometimes the snow falls. In the winter, we often go hungry but, in the spring, the hunters kill game again. And even in winter, there is much to do—the fires to be tended, the deerskins to be chewed and made soft."

"God gave you an immortal soul," I said. "Have you no feeling of it?"

She looked at me with her fey look—the look of a changeling.

"Now you talk like a medicine man," she said. She sighed. "They are very terrible and wonderful, of course. But a woman has other business."

"In God's name, what?" I said.

She opened her eyes wide.

"Why," she said, "to know how to work the skins and cook the food—yes, and plant the corn and the beans. You think that is hard work—but the English women I have talked to who come from the towns have harder. They live shut up in their towns like corn shut up in a pouch and they wear so many clothes the air never gets to their skin. They say it is a noble life, but I do not see how they bear it. We are often cold and hungry but, when there is food, we share it, and there is always the sky above and the earth beneath."

"But what is the end of it all?" I said, for it seemed to me she talked like a pagan or a child.

"Oh," she said, "to go to a man's lodge and lie by his side and bear his children. That is the end of it all."

"Would you have done that?" I said.

"Why, yes," she said. "Next year perhaps. Not this year, for they were not sure of the corn." She flushed, faintly. "He was a strong man, though older," she said. "He had plenty in his lodge and he had killed many enemies."

The thought made me desperate.

"I do not understand women," I said in a groaning voice. "I think I do not understand them at all."

I rose and walked up and down in front of the fire.

"Why are you walking up and down?" she said in an interested voice. "Are you thinking of your own enemies? Be content—I am sure you will kill many of them. You are strong and quick."

"No, child, no." I said. "I am thinking of your soul and my soul and—" I stopped and sat down beside her again.

"There is an old song," I said. "It is sung in my country of a man who was led astray. I do not know why I wish to sing it to you but I wish it."

So sitting beside her, by the campfire, in the great woods, I sang her the rough old ballad of Thomas the Rhymer, or as much of it as I could remember—how he met the Queen of Elfland and she took him where man should not go.

"'Now ye maun go wi' me' she said
'True Thomas, ye maun go wi' me;
And ye maun serve me seven years
Thro' weal or woe as chance may be.'"

I sang, and wondered as I sang, if it were the eildon-tree that, in truth, we sat beneath—the tree that is on the border of another land than ours. But when I reached the verse that says—

"It was mirk, mirk night, there was nae starlight,
They waded through red bluid to the knee"

—she nodded her head, and when I ended the song, she nodded again.

"That is a fine song," she said. "There is strong medicine in it. He was a strong chief—yet he did not have to go with her unless he wished it. It is so in some of our stories."

I could not speak but sat watching her. There was an intent and puzzled look upon her face. It seemed to me that I saw her from a great distance.

"There is something in the song," she said. "I cannot remember." She put her hand to her head. "I cannot remember," she said again. "But there was something in the song. I have heard it and another— another. The Queen was not clad in green—she was clad in scarlet. Do you know of that?"

She looked at me pitifully and eagerly, while her brows knitted, but I did not know how to help her. She struck her hands together and sang:

"The Queen was clad in scarlet
Her merry maids all in green,"

"Eh, feyther, I ken the tune—I'll not fail you."
I joined her in a low voice, greatly daring, but I do not know that she heard me, her face was so rapt and content.

"Ride hooly, hooly gentlemen," she sang,
"Ride hooly now wi' me."

Then, for a moment, her voice stumbled and faltered but only to come strongly and piercingly on the verse all Scotland knows.

"Yestreen the Queen had four Maries,
The night she'll hae but three;
There was Marie Seaton and Marie Beaton
And Marie Carmichael and me."

Then she gave a loud cry. "Carmichael—Mary Carmichael!" she said. "Hide yourself in the cupboard by the door, Jamie—the Indians are coming and feyther's head is all red!" and with the cry, her voice broke and she burst into a passion of tears. I held her in my arms, scarcely daring to breathe till it had passed for I knew that with that, name and recollection and Christian memory had come back to her.

Well, that is the wilderness-tale I have to tell you—a strange one enough, I think, though with no true sequel. I have talked since with a medical man in Philadelphia of much experience—he deems it probable that the sound of the Scots words and the lilt of the tune touched some hidden spring in the girl's mind and she knew, having long forgotten, that she was Mary Carmichael. It must have been a song that her father sang her oft.

I know myself that, from that moment, there was a certain change in her though I did not perceive it till afterwards. For the next day I fell ill of my fever again, and they tell me I was skin and bones when they brought me in to Carlisle.

When I came to myself again, and that was for more days than I care to count, she was sitting by my bedside. I could not account for the difference in her at first—then I saw she was decently dressed in Christian homespun, no longer in the gear of the savage. I should have rejoiced to see that and yet I did not.

MISS DENISON
ca. 1785
artist unknown

"You were singing, but I cannot remember the tune," I said, for those were the first words that came into my head.

"Hush," she said and smoothed my coverlet with her hand like any woman. "You have been very sick. You must rest awhile."

After I had grown stronger, I found from the woman in whose house I lay that she, Mary Carmichael, had come each day to nurse me. Also she had prepared certain draughts of leaves and herbs. I cannot remember drinking them but I fear they have entered forever into my veins.

She was not too changed, you understand. Even in the sad dress of the frontier, there was still a strangeness about her. But the changeling look had gone. She was very calm and kindly, sitting by my bedside, yet I knew I could not keep her or hold her, though I would dream at nights of bringing her back to Auchairn.

When I was quite strong again and she brought in the man named Henry—the strong, yellow-haired youth whose friend had been Little Bear—I knew that, too, was fitting. They were of a likeness and I was not of their likeness. When I had the barber in to powder my hair, I knew there was no likeness between us.

They were to be married next day, and they asked me to stand up with them, so I did so. The church, as it happened, was full, for the wedding of a captive caused great interest in the town. It is a plain, small church, but the minister was of the right persuasion.

Before that she thanked me very sweetly and civilly for teaching her her letters and for all that I had done. It was hard to bear, to have her thank me, yet now I am glad she did, for I shall remember it. The man thanked me also and wrung my hand. It was odd—he was shyer than she, in the church, though I had seen him friendly enough on the march. He had his rifle, his axe and a pack horse with some goods upon it. They were going to a place called the Forks of the Yadkin—it is many miles away in the rougher part of Virginia. From there, he thought they might venture some day to the wilds of a new land called Ken-tuck-e—a land full of game and grass where few white men had ever trod. It was odd to stand beside that man and, though one day I will be Auchairn, to feel myself poor beside him. Yet I have a good conceit of myself, as a rule.

The minister—a good man—made them an excellent and searching discourse on Christian wedlock. She listened to it attentively, but I have certain fears that she would have listened quite as prettily to the heathenish ravings of a medicine-man. Then they set off together, he and she. The last glimpse I had was of the silvery hair, as they topped the rise and began to go down. It was a clear day, not yet cold. He had his rifle in the crook of his arm—she walked a little behind him, leading the pack horse. She did not walk like a lady, but freely, and you could not hear her steps though the ground was covered with blown leaves.

The adventure has left me confused—I thought it might help my confusion to write it down. You will say it is all simple enough—that I fell in love with a rustic beauty for a few weeks, behaved like a gentleman and a Christian, and was glad to see her married off, in the end. That is true, perhaps, and yet there is something more. Even now, I cannot get the thought of those two people out of my mind. By now, no doubt, they will have reached the Forks of the Yadkin, and he will be making his clearing—there, in the utter wilderness that to them is home. It is there that their children will be born—or in some even wilder land. Yet was she very much of a woman, when she took me by the sleeve and said I wore pretty clothes.

They are not English or Scots—they are not German or Irish—it is a new nation they are making. We are deceived by the language, and even that begins to change on their tongues. Oh yes, I have been graciously received in fine houses in Philadelphia, but that was an imitation, as Bath is a little London. It is different, in the wilderness—and our Lords in Council have not fathomed it. As for me, I have taken the King's shilling, and some day I shall be Auchairn. Yet were it not so—I swear I should like to see what this stream called the Yadkin is like—I should like to see what children came of such a marriage. Aye, even did it mean the abandonment of all I have been.

You will think me daft to have such thoughts in my head—it may be I am not yet wholly recovered of the fever. It may also be that I shall never recover. We hear that the Government intends to close the Western frontiers to settlement—no doubt for good reasons of policy. But these people are not to be stayed, and I have seen them fight. Had they a Bouquet to lead them—well, this is all speculation. Yet I still keep thinking of my changeling. Aye, even had all things been otherwise, I could not have brought her back tamed, to be lady of Auchairn. And yet, she had nations in her eyes. ❧

Daniel Boone

Arthur Guiterman

Daniel Boone at twenty-one
Came with his tomahawk, knife, and gun
Home from the French and Indian War
To North Carolina and the Yadkin shore.
He married his maid with a golden band,
Builded his house and cleared his land;
But the deep woods claimed their son again
And he turned his face from the homes of men.
Over the Blue Ridge, dark and lone,
The Mountains of Iron, the Hills of Stone,
Braving the Shawnee's jealous wrath,
He made his way on the Warrior's Path.
Alone he trod the shadowed trails;
But he was lord of a thousand vales
As he roved Kentucky, far and near,
Hunting the buffalo, elk, and deer.
What joy to see, what joy to win,
So fair a land for his kith and kin,
Of streams unstained and woods unhewn!
"Elbow room!" laughed Daniel Boone.

On the Wilderness Road that his axemen made
The settlers flocked to the first stockade;
The deerskin shirts and the coonskin caps
Filed through the glens and the mountain gaps;
And hearts were high in the fateful spring
When the land said "Nay!" to the stubborn king.
While the men of the East of farm and town
Strove with the troops of the British Crown,
Daniel Boone from a surge of hate
Guarded a nation's westward gate.

DANIEL BOONE ESCORTING SETTLERS THROUGH THE CUMBERLAND GAP
1851–52
George Caleb Bingham

Down in the fort in a wave of flame
The Shawnee horde and the Mingo came,
And the stout logs shook in a storm of lead;
But Boone stood firm and the savage fled.
Peace! And the settlers flocked anew,
The farm lands spread, the town lands grew;
But Daniel Boone was ill at ease
When he saw the smoke in his forest trees.
"There'll be no game in the country soon.
Elbow room!" cried Daniel Boone.

Straight as a pine at sixty-five—
Time enough for a man to thrive—
He launched his bateau[1] on Ohio's breast
And his heart was glad as he oared it west;
There was kindly folk and his own true blood
Where great Missouri rolls his flood;
New woods, new streams, and room to spare,
And Daniel Boone found comfort there.
Yet far he ranged toward the sunset still,
Where the Kansas runs and the Smoky Hill,
And the prairies toss, by the south wind blown;
And he killed his bear on the Yellowstone.
But ever he dreamed of new domains
With vaster woods and wider plains;
Ever he dreamed of a world-to-be
Where there are no bounds and the soul is free.
At fourscore-five, still stout and hale,
He heard a call to a farther trail;
So he turned his face where the stars are strewn;
"Elbow room!" sighed Daniel Boone.
Down the Milky Way in its banks of blue
Far he has paddled his white canoe
To the splendid quest of the tameless soul—
He has reached the goal where there is no goal.

1 **bateau:** a flat-bottomed boat with oars

Now he rides and rides an endless trail
On the hippogriff[2] of the flaming tail
Or the horse of the stars with the golden mane,
As he rode the first of the blue-grass strain.
The joy that lies in the search he seeks
On breathless hills with crystal peaks;
He makes his camp on heights untrod,
The steps of the shrine, alone with God.
Through the woods of the vast, on the plains of space
He hunts the pride of the mammoth race
And the dinosaur of the triple horn,
The manticore[3] and the unicorn,
As once by the broad Missouri's flow
He followed the elk and the buffalo.
East of the sun and west of the moon,
"Elbow room!" laughs Daniel Boone.

Daniel Boone was a legend in his own time, alternately praised and cursed. He blazed the first road to Kentucky territory but also was charged with treason for his dealings with the Shawnee and the British. Acquitted of those charges, he later was bankrupted when his business as a land surveyor failed.

After paying his debts, Boone settled in Missouri. He died a respected man at the age of 85.

2 **hippogriff:** a legendary animal having the head of a griffin and the body of a horse

3 **manticore:** a legendary animal with the head of a man, the body of a lion, and the tail of a dragon

decent of 2 feet

Cascade of 14 feet 7 inches de...

47 feet 8 inches pitch

19 feet Pitch

rapid of 5 feet decent

Rapids & Cascades of abou...

10 feet decent

Deep rivere

...pid of 3 feet decent

...6 inches deceen

rapids of 18 feet decent

rapids of 6 feet decent

rapids of 18 feet decent

sulpher spring

5 feet fall

...tage River

Journals of the Lewis & Clark Expedition

Meriwether Lewis, William Clark, et al.

The object of your mission is to explore the Missouri river, & such principal stream of it, as, by its course and communication with the waters of the Pacific ocean, whether the Columbia, Oregon, Colorado or any other river may offer the most direct & practicable water communication across this continent for the purposes of commerce.

—President Thomas Jefferson's instructions to Captain Meriwether Lewis, June 20, 1803

ike the voyage of Columbus, the Lewis and Clark Expedition was an epic journey. For two years, four months, and nine days, two young men who had been friends in the army traveled with their companions over some 8,000 miles of wilderness.

Their journey came about after the U.S. bought the uncharted Louisiana Territory from France in 1803, which doubled the size of the nation. Joined by a crew of 42 men that came to be known as The Corps of Discovery, their task was to explore this land. Lewis was primed with crash courses in botany and astronomy so he could bring back news of the plants and weather of the unexplored lands.

The mission sparked the imagination of an entire country. Setting forth in three boats on the muddy Missouri River in the spring of 1804, the Corps opened up the American West. Excerpts from their journals follow—complete with their colorfully misspelled words. ❧

September 17, 1804

. . . this senery already rich pleasing and beatiful was still farther heightened by immence herds of Buffaloe, deer Elk and Antelopes which we saw in every direction feeding on the hills and plains. I do not think I exagerate when I estimate the number of Buffaloe which could be compre[hend]ed at one view to amount to 3000. my object was if possible to kill a female Antelope . . . we found the Antelope extreemly shye and watchfull–insomuch that we had been unable to get a shot at them; . . . I had this day an opportunity of witnessing the agility and the superior fleetness of this anamal which was to me really astonishing. . . .

—Captain Meriwether Lewis

As The Corps of Discovery headed north, they experienced a tense standoff with the Teton Sioux.

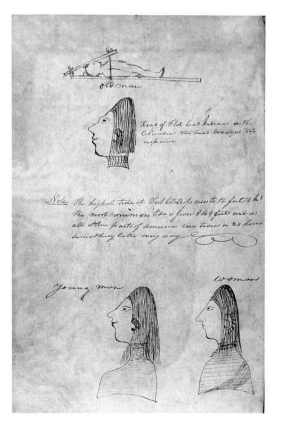

September 25, 1804

a clear and pleasant morning. al things made ready to receive the Band of the Souix nation of Indians, Called the Tribe of Tetons. about 10 o.C. A.M. they Came flocking in from boath Sides of the River. . . Capt Lewis & Capt Clark went out to Speak and treat with them. Gave the 3 Chiefs 3 niew meddals & 1 american flag Some knives & other Small articles of Goods & Gave the head chief the Black Buffalow a red coat & a cocked hat & feather &.C. likewise Some Tobacco. . . . they did not appear to talk much untill they had got the goods, and then they wanted more, and Said we must Stop with them or leave one of the pearogues[1] with them as that was what they expected. Capt Lewis Shewed them the air Gun. Shot it several times. . . then the Captains told them that we had a great ways to goe & that we did not wish to be detained any longer. the head chief the Black Buffaloe, Seized hold of the cable of the pearogue[1] and Set down. Capt Clark Spoke to all the party to Stand to their arms Capt Lewis who was on board ordered every man to his arms. the large Swivel [was] loaded immediately with 16 Musquet Ball in it the 2 other Swivels loaded well with Buck Shot [and] each of them manned. Capt Clark used moderation with them told them that we must and would go on and would go. . . . the chief Sayed . . . if we were to go on they would follow us and kill and take the whole of us by degrees or that he had another party or lodge above this

Lewis' and Clark's journals were filled with sketches of the people, plants, and animals they encountered.

1 **pearogue:** a misspelling of *pirogue*, a dugout boat similar to a canoe

[and] that they were able to destroy us. then Capt Clark told them that we were Sent by their great father the president of the U. S. and that if they mis-used us that he or Capt Lewis could by writing to him have them all distroyed as it were in a moment. . . . the chief then let go the Cable, and Sayed that he was Sorry to have us Go for his women and children were naked and poor and wished to Git Some Goods . . . Capt Clark took the chief and warriers on bord to Stay all night with them. . . . our Camp was on a wil-low Isl in the middle of the river, at our Starbord Side.

—Sergeant John Ordway

During their treacherous journey, the Corps members faced many difficulties. In an attempt to ward off mosquitoes, they slathered themselves in a mixture of tallow and lard. One of their worst problems was blowing sand.

April 24, 1805

The wind blew so hard during the whole of this day, that we were unable to move. . . . Soar eyes is a common complaint among the party. I believe it origenates from the immence quantities of sand which is driven by the wind from the sandbars of the river in such clouds that you are unable to discover the opposite bank of the river in many instances. . . . so penitrating is this sand that we cannot keep any arti-cle free from it; in short we are compelled to eat, drink, and breath it very freely.

—Captain Meriwether Lewis

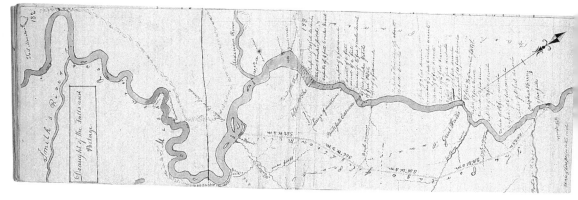

*Despite the hardships, there was joy. The Corps members thrilled
to their first glimpse of the snowcapped Rockies.*

May 26, 1805

while I viewed these mountains I felt a secret pleasure in finding myself
so near the head of the heretofore conceived boundless Missouri; but
when I reflected on the difficulties which this snowey barrier would
most probably throw in my way to the Pacific, and the sufferings and
hardships of myself and party in thim, it in some measure counterbal-
lanced the joy I had felt in the first moments in which I gazed on them;
but as I have always held it a crime to anticipate evils I will believe it a
good comfortable road untill I am compelled to believe differently.

—Captain Meriwether Lewis

*The Corps members often risked their lives while
negotiating unfamiliar terrain.*

June 7, 1805

It continued to rain almost without intermission last night and as I
expected we had a most disagreable and wrestless night. . . . In passing along the face of one of these bluffs today I sliped at a narrow pass
of about 30 yards in length and but for a quick and fortunate recovery
by means of my espontoon I should have been precipitated into the
river down a craggy pricipice of about ninety feet. I had scarcely
reached a place on which I could stand with tolerable safety even with
the assistance of my espontoon before I heard a voice behind me cry
out god god Capt. what shall I do on turning about I found it was
Windsor who had sliped and fallen ab[o]ut the center of this narrow
pass and was lying prostrate on his belley, with his wright hand arm
and leg over the precipice while he was holding on with the left arm
and foot as well as he could which appeared to be with much difficulty.
. . . I disguised my feelings and spoke very calmly to him and assured
him that he was in no kind of danger, to take the knife out of his belt
behind him with his wright hand and dig a hole with it in the face of
the bank to receive his wright foot which he did and then raised him-

A hand-drawn map by a member of the expedition

self to his knees; I then directed him to take off his mockersons and to come forward on his hands and knees holding the knife in one hand and the gun in the other this he happily effected and escaped.

—Captain Meriwether Lewis

Some historians credit Sacagewea, a Shoshone Indian, with greatly helping the mission through her knowledge of the land and her skill in communicating with Indian tribes. She came to serve as a guide for Lewis and Clark by accident—she had been kidnapped and sold to a French fur trader who was traveling with the Corps as an interpreter. She is referred to as "squar" in the entry below.

August 17, 1805

The Interpreter & Squar who were before me at Some distance danced for the joyful sight, and She made signs to me that they were her nation, (By sucking her fingers.) . . . The Great Chief of this nation proved to be the brother of the woman with us and is a man of Influence Sence & easey & reserved manners, appears to possess a great deel of Cincerity.

. . . every thing appeared to astonish those people. the appearance of the men, their arms, the Canoes, the Clothing my black Servent & the Segassity of Capt Lewis's Dog. . . . we made a number of enquires of those people about the Columbia River the Countrey game & [et]c. The account they gave us was verry unfavourable, that the River abounded in emence falls, one perticularly much higher than the falls of the Missouri & at the place the mountains Closed so Close that it was impracticable to pass, & that the ridge Continued on each Side of perpendicular Clifts inpenetratable, and that no Deer Elk or any game was to be found in that Countrey, aded to that they informed us that there was no timber on the river Sufficiently large to make Small Canoes, This information (if true is alarming) I deturmined to go in advance and examine the countrey, See if those dificueltes presented themselves in the gloomey picture in which they painted them, and if the river was practi[c]able and I could find timber to build Canoes,

. . . the Indians being so harrassed & compelled to move about in those rugid mountains that they are half Starved liveing at this time on berries & roots which they geather in the plains. Those people are not begerley but generous, only one has asked me for anything and he for powder

—2nd Lieutenant William Clark

During a dangerous overland trek to the Columbia River, several horses fell and the men nearly starved. Their luck turned with a relatively easy trip down the Columbia River and winter camp on the shores of the Pacific Ocean.

November 7, 1805

Great joy in camp we are in viuew of the Ocian, this great Pacific Octean which we been so long anxious to See. and the roreing or noise made by the waves brakeing on the rockey Shores (as I suppose) may be heard disti[n]ctly
—2nd Lieutenant William Clark

In 1806, Lewis and Clark—who had at one point been given up for lost by folks back home—joyfully returned to St. Louis. There, all one thousand of the residents lined the riverbanks, cheering for the homecoming of the rough-looking, buckskin-clad heroes. Their journey inspired many other adventurers to follow their footsteps. Their names are linked forever as the brave young partners who opened the American West.

Lewis and Clark recorded 178 plants and 122 animals that were new to science.

RESPONDING TO CLUSTER ONE

WHAT WERE EXPLORERS SEEKING?
THINKING SKILL ANALYZING

1. Reread Christopher Columbus' journal, as well as the September 25, 1804, and August 17, 1805, journal entries of the Lewis and Clark expedition. Use the chart below to **analyze** the reactions of Columbus, Meriwether Lewis, and William Clark, to Native Americans and the New World.

Explorer	Why explore?	Discoveries made	Result
Columbus			
Meriwether Lewis			
William Clark			

2. Imagine you are a Native American viewing the European explorers for the first time. Record your observations, using specific details. **Analyze** your reaction to their approach.

3. **Analyze** the narrator's attitude and feelings toward the girl in "The Captives." Why does she disturb him?

4. What does the repetition of the phrase "elbow room" in the poem "Daniel Boone" say about Boone and the American attitude toward the frontier?

Writing Activity: Future Exploration
Imagine you are in charge of exploring a previously undiscovered planet. Write instructions for your explorers. What should they do, touch, bring back? Make a list of five things they are to do and five things they are not to do. Use President Thomas Jefferson's instructions for the Lewis and Clark expedition as a guide, in addition to anything else you may have learned about exploratory missions in this cluster.

Good Instructions
• will begin with an explanation of the exploration's mission.
• will set rules and parameters for explorers.
• will end with a sentence of encouragement and inspiration for the explorers.

CLUSTER TWO

What Were the Effects of Manifest Destiny?

Thinking Skill COMPARING AND CONTRASTING

An Apache scout, ca. 1906, as photographed by Edward S. Curtis

Whig political banner ca. 1840, Terrance J. Kennedy

MANIFEST DESTINY

Christina Beck

Lewis and Clark opened up the west to settlement at the turn of the nineteenth century. By the 1840s, leaders and politicians used the phrase "Manifest Destiny" to justify American ownership of land all the way to the west coast, no matter who was there first.

The phrase sounded inspiring, but what did it mean? The words "manifest destiny" themselves mean "certain fate." In the nineteenth century, however, Manifest Destiny meant more. It meant that in the name of liberty, Americans claimed the right to extend not only their landholdings but also their way of life from coast to coast. Indians and the Hispanic rancheros of the southwest were decidedly not part of this plan. The thinking was that American democracy was so desirable that it should overrule existing ways of life.

How did the thinking behind Manifest Destiny begin? It may have begun when eighteenth-century trailblazers such as Daniel Boone were followed into the wilderness by early settlers. Feeling crowded, the trailblazers pushed ever farther west.

Another factor was a population explosion—bigger families meant more hands to share the work. The economic depressions of 1818 and 1839 bankrupted many who packed up their troubles in Conestoga wagons to start over in the West with cheap or free land. By the 1840s, immigrants from Europe and China joined the westward tide.

In this huge country with its enormously varied terrain, land has always been a powerful symbol for freedom. Perhaps land has never been a more powerful symbol, though, than it was during the era of Manifest Destiny as Americans pushed relentlessly westward to the coast. ☜

A Friend of the Indians

Joseph Bruchac

A man who was known
as a friend of the Indians
spoke to Red Jacket one day
about the good treatment
the Senecas enjoyed
from their white neighbors.

Red Jacket walked with him
beside the river, then suggested
they should sit together
on a log next to the stream.

They both sat down.
Then Red Jacket slid closer
to the man and said, "Move Over."

The man moved over, but when he did
Red Jacket again slid closer.
"Move Over," he said.

Three times this happened
until the man had reached
the end of the log near the water.
Then, once more, he was told,
"Move Over."

"But if I move further
I shall fall in the water,"
the man pleaded,
teetering on the edge.

Red Jacket replied,
"And even so you whites
tell us to move on when
no place is left to go."

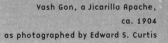

Vash Gon, a Jicarilla Apache,
ca. 1904
as photographed by Edward S. Curtis

Cherokee mother and child

TSALI OF THE CHEROKEES

Norah Roper as told to Alice Marriott

In the time when their troubles began, the ordinary Cherokees did not at first understand that anything was really wrong. They knew that their tribal chiefs traveled back and forth to the white man's place called Washington more often than they used to do. They knew that when the chiefs came back from that place there were quarrels in the tribal council.

Up in the hills and the back country, where the *Ani Keetoowah*—the true Cherokees—lived, word of the changes came more slowly than the changes themselves came to the valley Cherokees. Many of the hill people never left their farm lands, and those who did went only to the nearest trading post and back. Few travelers ever came into the uplands, where the mists of the Smokies[1] shut out the encroaching world.

So, when the news came that some of the chiefs of the Cherokees had touched the pen, and put their names or their marks on a paper, and agreed by doing so that this was no longer Cherokee country, the *Ani Keetoowah* could not believe what they heard. Surely, they said to each other, this news must be false. No Cherokee—not even a mixed-blood—would sign away his own and his people's lands. But that was what the chiefs had done.

Then the word came that the chiefs were even more divided among themselves, and that not all of them had touched the pen. Some were

---

1 **Smokies:** The Great Smoky Mountains in North Carolina and Tennessee

not willing to move away to the new lands across the Mississippi and settle in the hills around Fort Gibson, Oklahoma.

"Perhaps we should hang on," the *Ani Keetoowah* said to one another. "Perhaps we will not have to go away after all." They waited and hoped, although they knew in their hearts that hope is the cruelest curse on mankind.

One of the leaders of the *Ani Keetoowah* was Tsali. The white men had trouble pronouncing his name, so they called him "Charley" or "Dutch." Tsali was a full-blood, and so were his wife and their family. They were of the oldest *Keetoowah* Cherokee blood and would never have let themselves be shamed by having half-breed relatives.

Tsali and his four sons worked two hillsides and the valley between them, in the southern part of the hill country. Tsali and his wife and their youngest son lived in a log house at the head of the hollow. The others had their own homes, spread out along the hillsides. They grew corn and beans, a few English peas, squashes and pumpkins, tobacco and cotton, and even a little sugar cane and indigo.[2] Tsali's wife kept chickens in a fenced run away from the house.

The women gathered wild hemp[3] and spun it; they spun the cotton, and the wool from their sheep. Then they wove the thread into cloth, and sometimes in winter when their few cattle and the sheep had been cared for and the chickens fed and there was not much else to do, the men helped at the looms which they had built themselves. The women did all the cutting and the making of garments for the whole family.

Tsali and his family were not worldly rich, in the way that the chiefs and some of the Cherokees of the valley towns were rich. They had hardly seen white man's metal money in their lives. But Tsali's people never lacked for food, or good clothing, or safe shelter.

* * *

The missionaries seldom came into the uplands then. Tsali took his sons and their wives, and his own wife, to the great dance ground where the seven *Keetoowah* villages gathered each month at the time of the full moon. There they danced their prayers in time to the beating

---

2 **indigo:** a plant used to make blue dye

3 **hemp:** a plant used to make rope and cloth

of the women's terrapin-shell leg rattles,[4] around and around the mound of packed white ashes on top of which bloomed the eternal fire that was the life of all the Cherokees.

The occasional missionaries fussed over the children. They gave them white men's names, so by Tsali's time everyone had an Indian name and an English one. The Cherokees listened to the missionaries politely, for the missionaries were great gossips, and the Cherokees heard their news and ignored the rest of their words.

"You will have to go soon," said one white preacher to Tsali, "there's no hope this time. The lands have all been sold, and the Georgia troopers are moving in. You'll have to go west."

"We'll never leave," Tsali answered. "This is our land and we belong to it. Who could take it from us—who would want it? It's hard even for us to farm here, and we're used to hill farming. The white men wouldn't want to come here—they'll want the rich lands in the valleys, if the lowland people will give them up."

"They want these hills more than any other land," the missionary said. He sounded almost threatening. "Don't you see, you poor ignorant Indian? They are finding gold—gold, man, gold—downstream in the lower *Keetoowah* country. That means that the source of the gold is in the headwaters of the rivers that flow from here down into the valleys. I've seen gold dust in those streams myself."

"Gold?" asked Tsali. "You mean this yellow stuff?" And he took a buckskin pouch out of the pouch that hung from his sash, and opened it. At the sight of the yellow dust the pouch contained, the missionary seemed to go a little crazy.

"That's it!" he cried. "Where did you get it? How did you find it? You'll be rich if you can get more."

"We find it in the rivers, as you said," Tsali replied. "We gather what we need to take to the trader. I have this now because I am going down to the valley in a few days, to get my wife some ribbons to trim her new dress."

"Show me where you got it," the missionary begged. "We can all be rich. I'll protect you from the other white men, if you make me your partner."

"No, I think I'd better not," said Tsali thoughtfully. "My sons are my partners, as I was my father's. We do not need another partner, and, as

---

4 **terrapin-shell leg rattles:** rattles made of turtle shells

long as we have our old squirrel guns, we do not need to be protected. Thank you, but you can go on. We are better off as we are."

* * *

The missionary coaxed and threatened, but Tsali stood firm. In the end, the white man went away, without any gold except a pinch that Tsali gave him, because the missionary seemed to value the yellow dust even more than the trader did.

Then it was time to go to the trading post. When Tsali came in the store, the trader said to him, "Well, Chief, glad to see you. I hear you're a rich man these days."

"I have always been a rich man," Tsali answered. "I have my family and we all have our good health. We have land to farm, houses to live in, food on our tables, and enough clothes. Most of all, we have the love in our hearts for each other and our friends. Indeed, you are right. We are very rich."

"That's one way of looking at it," said the trader, "but it isn't what I was thinking about. From what I hear, there's gold on your land. You've got a gold mine."

"A gold man?" repeated Tsali. "I never heard of a gold man."

"No!" shouted the trader. "A gold *mine*, I said. A place where you can go and pick up gold."

"Oh, that!" Tsali exclaimed. "Yes, we have some places like that on our land. Here's some of the yellow dust we find there."

And he opened the pouch to show the trader. The trader had seen pinches of Tsali's gold dust before, and taken it in trade, without saying much about it. Now he went as crazy as the missionary. "Don't tell anybody else about this, Charley," he whispered, leaning over the counter. "We'll just keep it to ourselves. I'll help you work it out, and I'll keep the other white men away. We'll all be rich."

"Thank you," said Tsali, "but I don't believe I want to be rich that way. I just want enough of this stuff to trade you for ribbons and sugar."

"Oh, all right," answered the trader sulkily, "have it your own way. But don't blame me if you're sorry afterwards."

"I won't blame anybody," said Tsali, and bought his ribbon.

A month later, when the Georgia militia came riding up the valley to Tsali's house, the missionary and the trader were with them. The men all stopped in front of the house, and Tsali's wife came out into the dogtrot, the open-ended passage that divided the two halves of the house and made a cool breezeway where the family sat in warm weather. She spoke to the men.

"Won't you come in and sit down?"

"Where's the old man?" the militia captain asked.

"Why, he's working out in the fields," said Amanda. "Sit down and have a cool drink of water while I send the boy for him."

"Send the boy quickly," the captain ordered. "We'll wait in our saddles and not trouble to get down."

"All right, if you'd rather not," Amanda said. "Do you mind telling me why you're here?"

"We're here to put you off this place," said the captain. "Haven't you heard? This isn't Cherokee land any more; the chiefs signed it over to the government, and now it's open for settlement. One or the other of these two gentlemen will probably claim it."

"They can't do that!" Amanda protested. "It's our land—nobody else's. The chiefs had no right to sign it away. My husband's father worked this place, and his father before him. This is our home. This is where we belong."

"No more," said the captain. "You belong in the removal camps down by the river, with the rest of the Indians. They're going to start shipping the Cherokees west tomorrow morning."

Amanda sat down on the bench in the dogtrot, with her legs trembling under her. "All of us?" she asked.

"Every one of you."

"Let me call my son and send him for his daddy," Amanda said.

"Hurry up!"

Amanda went into the house, calling to the boy, who was just fourteen and had been standing, listening, behind the door. She gave him his father's old squirrel gun, and he sneaked his own blowgun and darts and slid out the back of the house. Amanda went back to the dogtrot and sat and waited. She sat there and waited, while the missionary, the trader, and the captain quarreled about which of their wives should cook in her kitchen. She let them quarrel and hoped her men were all right.

Tsali and his older sons were working at the overhill corn field, when the boy came panting up, and told them what had happened.

"Is your mother all right?" Tsali asked.

"She was when I left," the boy answered.

"We'll hide in the woods till they're gone," Tsali told his older sons. "If they find us, they'll have to kill us to put us off this land."

"What about the women?" the oldest son asked.

"They'll be all right," Tsali answered. "Your mother's a quick-thinking woman; she'll take care of them. If we can hide in the caves by the river till dark, we'll go back then and get them."

They slipped away into the woods, downhill to the river, taking the boy with them, although he offered to go back and tell the white men he couldn't find his father.

All afternoon Amanda waited. Her daughters-in-law saw the strange men and horses in front of the big house and came to join her. At dusk, the captain gave up and ordered his men to make camp in the front yard. "We'll wait here until the men come back," he said.

With the white men camped all around the house, the women went into the kitchen and barred all the doors. It was a long time before the campfires made from the fence pickets ceased to blaze and began to smolder. It was a longer time until the women heard it—a scratch on the back door, so soft and so light that it would have embarrassed a mouse. Amanda slid back the bar, and Tsali and his sons slipped into

Cherokee family outside of their cabin in North Carolina

the darkened room. There was just enough moonlight for them to make out each other's shapes.

"We came to get you," Tsali said. "Come quickly. Leave everything except your knives. Don't wait a minute."

Amanda and her daughters-in-law always wore their knives at their belts, so they were ready. One at a time, Tsali last, the whole family crept out of their home and escaped into the woods.

In the morning, when the white men stretched and scratched and woke, the *Ani Keetoowah* were gone.

* * *

It was spring, and the weather was warm, but the rain fell and soaked the Cherokees. They had brought no food, and they dared not fire a gun. One of the daughters-in-law was pregnant, and her time was close. Amanda was stiff and crippled with rheumatism. They gathered wild greens, for it was too early for berries or plums, and the men and boy trapped small animals and birds in string snares the women made by pulling out their hair and twisting it.

Day by day, for four weeks, the starving family listened to white men beating through the woods. The Cherokees were tired and cold and hungry, but they were silent. They even began to hope that in time the white men would go away and the Indians would be safe.

It was not to be. One trooper brought his dog, and the dog caught the human scent. So the dog, with his man behind him, came sniffing into the cave, and Tsali and his family were caught before the men could pick up their loaded guns.

The militiaman shouted, and other white men came thudding through the woods. They tied the Cherokee men's hands behind them and bound them all together along a rope. The militiamen pushed Tsali and his sons through the woods. The women followed, weeping.

At last, they were back at their own house, but they would not have recognized it. The troopers had plundered the garden, and trampled the plants they didn't eat. The door from the kitchen into the dogtrot hung askew, and the door to the main room had been wrenched off its hinges. Clothes and bedding lay in filthy piles around the yard. What the militiamen could not use, they ruined.

"Oh, my garden!" cried Amanda, and, when she saw the scattered feathers, "Oh, my little hens!"

"What are you going to do with us?" Tsali demanded.

"Take you down to the river. The last boat is loading today. There's still time to get you on it and out of here."

"I—will—not—go," Tsali said quietly. "You—nor you—nor you—nobody can make me go."

"Our orders are to take all the Cherokees. If any resist, shoot them."

"Shoot me, then!" cried Tsali. The captain raised his rifle.

"Stop!" Amanda screamed. She stepped over beside her husband. "If you shoot, shoot us both," she ordered. "Our lives have been one life since we were no older than our boy here. I don't want to go on living without my husband. And I cannot leave our home any more than he can. Shoot us both."

The four sons stepped forward. "We will die with our parents," the oldest one said. "Take our wives to the boat, if that is the only place where they can be safe, but we stay here." He turned to his wife and the other young women.

"That is my order as your husband," Tsali's son said. "You must go away to the west and make new lives for yourselves while you are still young enough to do so." The wives sobbed and held out their arms, but the husbands turned their backs on the women. "We will stay with our parents," all the young men said.

The young boy, too, stood with his brothers, beside his father. "Let this boy go," Tsali said to the white men. "He is so young. A man grows, and plants his seed, and his seed goes on. This is my seed. I planted it. My older sons and I have had our chances. They will leave children, and their names will never be forgotten. But this boy is too young. His seed has not ripened for planting yet. Let him go to care for his sisters on the way to the west."

"Very well," said the captain. "He can't do much harm if he does live." He turned to two militiamen. "Take the boy and the young women away," he ordered. "Keep them going till they come to the boats, and load them on board."

The young women and the boy, stunned and silenced, were driven down the road before they could say goodbye, nor would the troopers let them look back. Behind them, as they started on the long main road, they heard the sound of the shots. ❧

TOUCHING THE SKIRTS OF HEAVEN

Mary Moore

Whether the early pioneers were running away from something (debts, ruined reputations, family problems) or seeking something (land, wealth, adventure), the enormous open spaces beyond the Missouri River offered them their best chance at a brand new life.

By the middle of the 19th century, much of the fertile land east of the Missouri had already been claimed. The goldminers and railroad workers made their way westward to the mountains or Pacific coast, but land-hungry pioneers looked toward the newly opened Kansas and Nebraska Territories.

The Homestead Act of 1862 spurred western settlement dramatically. To those who crossed the prairies empty-handed it must have seemed like a dream come true: 160 "free" acres for any settler who put up a dwelling and invested five continuous years developing the property.

Germans, Irish, Scandinavians, and others came in droves to take advantage of the land offer. Wagon trains, railroads and steamers ferried homesteaders to the massive grassy expanses of the Plains frontier.

Few pioneers were prepared for their first views of the Great Plains, which seemed to stretch out forever. The famous 19th-century writer Robert Louis Stevenson declared, "It was a world almost without a feature; an empty sky, an empty earth; front and back, the line of railway stretched from horizon to horizon, like a cue across a billiard-board; on either hand, the green plain ran till it touched the skirts of heaven."

The Rawding family, Nebraska, 1886

Grasses which had been saddle-high on the prairie diminished to waist or knee-length as a traveler approached the true plains; along with the wildflowers, they created a vivid and richly textured carpet over some of the most fertile soil in the world.

Landmarks were few. There might be some chalky bluffs alongside the rivers, or a rare outcropping of rock, but even trees were unusual on the arid, grass-choked plains. A cottonwood stand was a welcome sight on the horizon, signaling shade and a nearby source of water.

Stevenson also noted the sheer noisiness of the grasshoppers, whose "incessant chirp" sounded over his locomotive like "the winding up of countless clocks and watches." To him and others, the Great Plains seemed as overwhelming as the sea. Without trees or buildings to break its force, the wind drove some of the settlers half-mad.

As white Europeans came, they grabbed up lands previously set aside for Native Americans. Treaties were broken with impunity. The anger of the Indians grew until it exploded in 1864, with the Sioux and Cheyenne tribes staging a violent uprising that closed over 400 miles of the Oregon Trail for several weeks. But the pioneers kept coming, and as they came, they claimed the grazing land of the buffalo, so key to the Plains Indians' survival.

By the end of the 1880s, the buffalo would nearly be extinct, and most of the Indians resettled, their semi-nomadic way of life ended forever. Many tribes were ravaged by such "white men's diseases" as smallpox.

The pioneers' first step after marking off their new land was to erect a house. These were often dug into the sides of hills or made of sod strips, stacked like bricks. Sod was good for insulation, if not so handy at keeping out rodents, snakes, or rain.

Nothing had prepared the newcomers for the extremity of the plains weather. There were blizzards, droughts, tornadoes, raging thunderstorms, and dust gales. Torrential rains fell on top of drought-hardened earth and created flash floods, washing tons of rich topsoil into rivers and streams. Temperatures plummeted to fifty degrees below zero in winter, and in summer the plains baked, with temperatures of over 100 degrees. In addition to the violent climate, plagues of grasshoppers might swoop in and devour the crops in a matter of hours.

Those settlers who survived were either exceptionally hardy or plain lucky. In 1869–70 the most common causes of pioneer death were pneumonia, fever, freezing, gunshot wounds, and consumption. They also died from lightning, horse kicks, alcoholism, and sunstrokes.

If the elements, illness, or accidents weren't challenge enough, the pioneers faced the daunting prospect of tilling the unforgiving land. The plains' tough and wiry root growth cracked many a plow

A sod-breaking plow

and many a farmer's spirit. Some settlers resorted to hacking the ground with an ax and dropping seeds into the cracks. Eventually the John Deere plow—one made of sinewy steel instead of rigid iron—would be invented to help till the tough prairie sod.

A family's survival weighed as heavily on pioneer women as on their menfolk. From sunup to sundown there was little relief from the hard work. Along with sowing and harvesting the crops—typically corn and wheat—the women had to clean, cook, and raise young children. Their meagre resources made this a daily challenge.

Wardrobes might consist of a few calico dresses, hand-me-downs from out East, pants made of feed sacks, and coats from buffalo hides, everything much worn and patched. For extra warmth in the harsh winters, blankets and pockets were sometimes stuffed with potatoes or rocks hot from the hearth. Sewing was done by the light of a simple grease lamp made from a saucer of animal fat, its wick a nail with a twist of flannel.

Meals were often monotonous—beans, cornbread, bacon, wild game, and if a family was lucky enough to live by water, fresh fish. Instead of sugar, they would often use sorghum molasses. If they were unable to get hold of coffee or tea, they might resort to brewed parched

corn. On the plus side, there were often wild berries and grapes and plums for pies and cobblers.

Life revolved around a family's basic needs, and rare were the luxuries—a skein of bright new yarn, an orange, a book. For news, they relied on traveling preachers and salesmen, infrequent letters from back East, and budding newspapers. Church services provided a chance for socializing and a respite from the endless toil. Dances were important to many communities, the only requirements being a fiddler and a dance floor.

But the emotional isolation was a heavy burden to many pioneer women, who had left behind mothers, sisters, and friends. They not only lacked company, but also lost an important source of information about health and household matters. Some women called their diaries their "dearest friends," relating in them their homesickness as well as fears for their family's safety.

Children were cherished, but also highly valued for the amount of work they could contribute to a homestead. Often their physical size and capacity for hard work counted more than their age. Few were the five-year-olds who didn't have some regular chores to perform, such as collecting buffalo chips for fuel or drawing water.

Top; Mabel Williams brings water to the threshing crew on her Minnesota homestead, 1909.

Middle: A North Dakota quilting bee, ca. 1890

Bottom: Gathering buffalo 'chips' for fuel

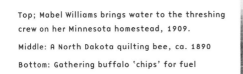

"Pioneer spirit" is a phrase familiar to most Americans. It calls to mind our ancestors' fierce self-reliance, their ability to work hard and withstand adversity. It should also be synonymous with hope—hope big enough to touch the plains sky. As the turn-of-the-century writer Carl Becker noted, "Idealism must always prevail on the frontier, for the frontier, whether geographical or intellectual, offers little hope to those who see things as they are. To venture into the wilderness, one must see it, not as it is, but as it will be." ◈

McGUFFEY'S
FIFTH
ECLECTIC
READER

REVISED
EDITION

AMERICAN · BOOK · COMPANY
NEW YORK CINCINNATI · CHICAGO

A prairie schoolhouse in Kansas, 1892

The Courtship

George Ella Lyon

When Sickly Jim Wilson's first wife died
he tried to carry on
keep house and farm his scrabbly land
and it like to broke him.
All them kids were too old to stay put
and too young to carry water. There was no one
to cook, wash, or sew, no one but Sickly Jim
and him the same body who must milk the cow
and plant the scanty hay. Soon he saw
he had to have another wife.

He considered the prospects on the creek,
listed them according to his favor:
Widow Jones, Miss Creech, the oldest Phillips girl,
and even Mossie Maggem. The thought of Mossie
made his belly cold, but next morning he set out.

Widow Jones was stringing beans on her hillside
porch. He rode right up to the rail.
"Morning Miz Jones. How are you now?"
"Working steady," was her answer,
"and how about yourself?" "Not faring well,

not faring well at all. If I'm to farm
and raise my kids, I've got to have a helpmeet.
That's why I'm here. It looks to me
like you might be the one. What do you say?"

She studied him, walked to the edge of the porch.
"I didn't think wives were got
the way a man gets pigs or harness.
I thought it usually took a little time
and a feller got off his horse."
"You know, Miz Jones, I mean no offense
but time's a thing I've run short of.

I've got babies crying at home
and so I speak out plain."
"Well give me the day. You come back
 around suppertime for my answer."
"No ma'am. I need a wife before that."
He looked at the paper in his hand.
"You're the first on my list, but if you
can't oblige, I'll be off to try Miss Creech."

He settled his hat, turned his horse,
and was almost out of the yard
when she called to him, "I've given it thought.
It's clear I'm the wife you need.
Hold till Sunday and I'll marry you."
And that's just what she did.

THE HOMESTEADER'S WIFE
1916
Harvey Dunn
South Dakota Art Museum Collection

END OF THE TRAIL

Jim Kjelgaard

They lay together by the trail—a broken axle, a dead ox, and an elaborately carved chest of drawers filled with household goods. Jim Clyman swung off his horse to examine them. The little brown dog that had been running beside him edged curiously up to sniff at the ox, and the horse blew through its nostrils. Jim Clyman reached up with his left hand to scratch the gray stubble on his chin. He looked westward, where the ominous spears that were the peaks of the Sierra Nevada Mountains arched endlessly to reach the sky, and studied the nest of clouds that were gathering over them. A broken axle, a dead ox, and a chest of drawers. . . . The little brown dog wagged his tail at him, and Jim Clyman spoke as he would have to a man.

"There's gonna be trouble up ahead, Bub."

The brown spaniel reared with both front paws against his master's thigh, and shoved his nose into the cupped hand. The old mountain man stroked the dog's ears absently, and spat into the rutted trail. There was going to be trouble, sure enough, although not this time from the Indians. The Arikaras, Arapahos, and Blackfeet had been tamed back in the early twenties, when the mountain men and the trappers had been the only ones to hit the trails west of the Missouri. Tenderfeet now traveled those paths which the feet—and the blood— of the mountain men had marked. Now tenderfeet needn't fear the Indians—anyhow, not very much. But they didn't take into proper account the much more savage enemies of mountains and distance and weather with which they had to cope in this year of 1844, when every tenderfoot, all his brothers and sisters, sons and daughters, uncles, aunts, and grandparents seemed to be either on the way to California or Oregon, or obsessed with the idea that they must soon start.

A broken axle, a dead ox, and a chest of drawers filled with household goods. . . .

Jim Clyman spat again into the rut, and did some thinking. There had been six wagons in this party ahead of him when he left Fort Bridger, back in Wyoming. Their trail had freshened considerably just after he left the Humboldt Sink. Now five of them had gone on, and might already be over the divide above Truckee Lake. The sixth had broken down; its occupants had taken time out to make another axle, and the cow that had been tied to the back of the wagon had been yoked in to take the dead ox's place. The team that now pulled this wagon was a very tired one. Women, Jim Clyman reflected, would hang on to their household goods until the last gasp. They'd keep the chest unless it just had to be thrown out so the wagon could be lightened and half-dead cattle could still stagger on toward the land of promise, the milk-and-honey land of California.

The old mountain man looped the horse's reins over his arm and started to walk along the trail, his eyes on the ground. Trotting placidly beside him, the little brown dog waved his tail and gave all his attention to snuffling through the rut in which he walked.

The long trail to the promised land, Jim Clyman thought, was surely marked with heartache. The path taken by these people was strewn with dead oxen, and graves, and broken wagons, and chests, and tools, clear back to the old homes from which they had come. Why did they get themselves a yoke of oxen, or a team of mules and a covered wagon, cast everything else aside, and hit the long stretch clear to the West? Jim Clyman answered his own question aloud.

"I know why, Bub," he said to the dog.

Back in New England homesteads, while battling their way through drifts to feed cattle, men thought of perpetually green fields where cattle could graze all winter. Or, while guiding a plow through stubborn, rock-strewn earth, they dreamed of soft black soil where plows never bucked. Or women in storm-lashed prairie huts conjured up images of flowers blooming at Christmas, or zephyr-soft breezes instead of blizzards. The West was a rich and sunny land where every woman was a queen and every man a king. It was thus that these people had talked to themselves and, talking, convinced themselves that they should go to Oregon or California. But they were deluding themselves and they knew it. Deep in their hearts they were aware that they had to go West for the same reason that Columbus had to sail for America. All about was sameness, and unchanging ideas, and routine, and satisfied people who were content to cope with the world they knew. But if there was something new to discover, an opportunity to be seized, a challenge to be met, *they* wanted to do it.

"That's the answer, Bub," Jim Clyman said.

He sighed and mounted his horse. People who blindly obeyed a beckoning finger that bent in their direction were always getting into messes, and this was going to be a bad one if somebody didn't come along to get them out. There were two men, a woman, and two children with the wagon ahead, and they were walking. He had found out that much while he studied their trail. Again he looked at the piled masses of clouds over the mountains, and shook his head.

It was a long, cruel trail that the immigrants had followed. Along it many a man, woman, and child, bereft of their own horses or wagons, had been refused permission to use someone else's. They had had to walk, and it was a singular thing that they had nearly always walked toward the magic lodestone[1] that drew them to the West. They had walked until they died—except for those very few who had walked clear to California. But all the luck in the world had been on the side of those who had finally made it.

And the cruelest part of the entire trail was the divide above Truckee Lake. It was only a year ago that Jim Clyman had helped another train of six wagons get over it. They had hitched four span of oxen to a single wagon, and they had strained up the slope until some of them had died from the terrific strain. Other oxen had been brought to replace the dead ones, and behind the wagon men and women had pushed. But that had been a train with oxen to spare, and no snow had yet fallen on the slopes.

Jim Clyman spurred his horse, and the animal broke into a little trot. His old friend, Caleb Greenwood, had been guiding that other train.

---

1 **lodestone:** something that attracts strongly

Most of the mountain men, now that it was no longer profitable to trap beaver, guided immigrants on the California or Oregon Trail. Caleb had been seventy-nine last year, but after they had finally come down from the mountains he had taken his gun and gone back up to get himself a mess of bear meat. The mush-and-milk food of the wagons, he had said, had run him down seriously. Jim Clyman smiled in recollection.

* * *

A day and a half later he rode his horse into Truckee Meadows and saw what he had known he would see there.

A fifteen-year-old boy, dressed in homespun and carrying a rifle, turned to stand beside the trail when he heard the horse. The little brown spaniel padded forward to meet him, and the boy stretched out a hand to stroke the dog's ears. The mountain man reined in his horse and dismounted.

"Howdy, Son. My name's Jim Clyman."

The boy tossed back his head, to fling the long, straight hair out of his eyes, and continued to tickle the dog's ears. "I'm Nathan Parker," he said. "I'm afraid you're in a bad way, Mr. Clyman."

"So?"

"You can't get over the divide. We tried it. We drove the three oxen and a cow up ahead of us to break a path. But the snow's too deep to go on. We stayed on the slope all night, and it snowed. The next morning we couldn't go on at all. We had to come back down and build a camp to spend the winter in."

"What happened to the oxen and the cow?"

"We got the cow back down—she hadn't been hitched for a long pull. But the oxen died right there in the snow and are all covered up now."

Jim Clyman writhed inwardly. You could always trust a tenderfoot to get himself into trouble, and then to make it worse with his own foolishness. A mountain man, knowing the divide to be snowed under, never would have taken the oxen up in the first place. A party aiming to winter had to have food, and the weather-wise game had already gone from these heights. Three oxen would have lasted five people a long time. But they were gone, and there was only the cow left.

"Got any grub in your wagon, Nate?" he asked.

"Not very much." The boy flushed with pleasure. A man, evidently one who understood this country, had called him Nate and was asking him questions. "All we got is just a little flour and beans, and Mr. Cressman's got those."

"Who's Mr. Cressman?"

"The man travelin' with us. It was really his flour. He owns the cow, too."

"Looks like Mr. Cressman aims to have vittles for a spell," Jim Clyman muttered. "Who else is along?"

"My Uncle George and Aunt Kate—their name's Parker, too. Uncle George is out huntin'. Then there's my little cousin, Ann. She's almost four. Are you goin' to stay with us?"

"I dunno just what's to be done, Sonny. S'pose we toss a stick in the air and see how she lands. I got a few blocks of pemmican[2] in my saddlebags, and it looks like we're goin' to need 'em."

They walked together up the trail, the little brown dog frisking ahead of them. A cold blast of air surged down from the top of the mountains. A few scattered flakes of snow trailed on the wings of the wind, and the angry brood of clouds glowered at them. Jim Clyman smelled wood smoke and a moment later they came within sight of a broken-down wagon and two brush tepees built at the base of a huge pine. Beside one of the shelters hung the freshly butchered carcass of a cow.

"I'll bet that'll be Cressman's dugout," Clyman grunted.

"Yep. He won't—"

Nate was interrupted by a woman who came out of the other side. She was tall, with clear blue eyes that were set far apart. The little girl who clung to her skirt was a tiny image of her mother. Jim Clyman nodded respectfully.

"Howdy, ma'am."

"Oh—hello. I had hardly expected—"

Nathan Parker said, "It's Mr. Jim Clyman, Aunt Kate. I found him riding up the trail. Uncle George get anything to eat?"

"He's not back yet." The woman looked questioningly at him, then down at the little girl. She hesitated.

Jim Clyman understood. On the road to California you were always welcome at any camp—so long as there was plenty of food in it. He reached into his saddlebag, got one of the pemmican blocks, and cut it

---

2 **pemmican:** an Indian food of dried meat pounded fine and mixed with melted fat

into two with his knife. Half of it, and the three remaining blocks, he slipped into the spacious pocket of his jacket. The little dog looked up pleadingly, but his owner looked away from him, at the woman.

"I'm right glad to know you, ma'am. Here. There's a lot of git in pemmican. Why don't you sort of cook up a meal for the little girl and yourself?"

The woman looked down again, and when she raised her head, tears brimmed in her eyes. Clyman looked away, pretending not to hear the thanks that she called after him, and walked over to the tree where the butchered cow hung. As he reached up for his knife for a piece of the meat, a warning voice came from the other shelter.

"Leave it alone."

The little dog backed against his legs, growling, and Jim Clyman stopped, knife in hand, to look at the stocky, dark-haired man who emerged from the other shelter.

"I'll bet you're Cressman."

"I'm Cressman, and that's my beef. Leave it alone."

Without seeming to move fast, the mountain man took three steps forward and dug the point of his knife into Cressman's pudgy stomach. His voice was mild but steady.

"It's camp meat and I'm takin' charge of it. I'm takin' the flour, too."

"You are not!"

"If you want to argue the point, we'll fight it out here and now and see who's gonna be boss."

Cressman muttered belligerently, but without looking at him again Jim Clyman cut off a piece of the beef, walked past the other into the brush shelter, and picked up the small keg with the few pounds of flour in it. Nathan Parker padded beside him as he strode away.

"He'll be mad at you!" he said in an awed voice.

"Well doggone, I've went and made somebody mad! Take this meat and the flour in to your Aunt Kate. The flour's for whoever needs it most, and I'm sayin' who needs it. Tell her to have a good hot stew ready for your uncle when he comes back."

The boy disappeared in the shelter, and Clyman unsaddled his horse. He rubbed the animal's nose a moment, then stood back and shot it through the head. An almost inaudible sigh escaped him. It had been a good horse, a faithful and intelligent horse. But when people's lives were in the balance a horse didn't count.

He sighed again. Of all the dang fools ever created, a mountain man was probably the dangdest. He and the horse and the dog could have gone over the divide. But only the most abysmal fool would think of coming into a camp of stranded immigrants, taking charge of it, and trying to take them over, too.

He had butchered the horse and was hanging it up when he saw a man emerge from the pine trees and walk through the steadily falling snow. Except for his rifle, he was empty-handed. Clyman pretended not to see, until a voice spoke from behind him.

"Hello, stranger."

"Why, howdy," Clyman said, turning as if in surprise. "You must be George Parker."

"That's right."

He was a thin man with pale blond hair and a hesitant manner. The mountain man's heart sank. It was certainly going to be a mismated crew that left this camp to go over the divide. Kate and George Parker, two sensitive, high-strung people with a fine native courage but no experience. Cressman, a selfish man ready to turn beast whenever that was expedient. A little girl who, at the best, would be an encumbrance, and a fifteen-year-old boy. He looked again at the blond man. George Parker seemed as though he'd be all right so long as he didn't have to face any difficult decisions, and then make them himself.

"Say, George," he said, "bring your wife, Nate, Cressman, and the little girl out here, will you? We got to have a powwow."

He stood near the place where he had butchered the horse, and the little brown dog came up to nuzzle his hand. He waited until the stranded wagoners were gathered about him, then addressed himself to George Parker. "How'd the huntin' go, George?"

Parker flushed. "I guess I'm not very good. I couldn't even see any game."

The mountain man shook his head grimly. "There ain't any to see; it's all gone down inta the valleys, where food's easier to get. So we'd starve to death if we tried to winter here. We got to go over the divide."

For a moment there was silence, as each in turn pondered this information.

"What assurance is there that we can do it?" Kate Parker asked.

"None. None a tall. The only sure thing is we'll starve if we don't do it."

He saw that pronouncement hit home with all the impact of a bullet. These tenderfeet wanted to go to California, not to starve. And they'd follow anybody who talked as though he were able to take them there, even though they had never seen him before today.

"I'm ready," Cressman growled.

"Well," George Parker said, looking at his wife, "well, I guess we'd better try."

"It looks," Clyman said deliberately, "like there ain't a vote ag'in it. We got more meat here than we can carry, and I want everybody to eat's much as they can before we start. Even if you got to stuff it down, do that. Mrs. Parker, save most of the flour for the little girl. George, I'll want your wagon spokes."

"What for?"

"For snowshoes. Spokes are good frames, and I'll lace 'em with hide. You and Cressman get in all the wood you can and take a big passel of meat inta the shelters. This snow's gonna fall hard, and we can't start till it's over."

* * *

It snowed hard for eight days—at first soft, feathery flakes, and then hard, crystalline ones that piled on top of the shelters and dribbled through the cracks in them until more snow added itself to that already there and stopped up the cracks. It piled up on the pine branches until they became overloaded and spilled their burdens. Driven by the wind, it formed long, curling drifts against every obstruction. And, when the storm finally passed, threatening clouds still hung over the divide.

During those eight days Jim Clyman, Nate, and the two Parkers had worked shaping the wheel spokes into snowshoe frames, scraping the hair from the horsehide and cowhide, slicking them into thin strips, drying these before the fire, and lacing the dried strips across the frames. Snow was piled high about the shelter, but the fire lit the interior, and sent its blue smoke climbing up through the smoke hole in the roof, which was kept open by poking a long stick up through it. The kettle bubbled constantly, melting snow for drinking water and simmering endless stews. Mealtime was any time anyone felt like eating. They could afford to be prodigal with their food when they could not possibly carry it all with them, and every ounce they ate now added to their strength.

On the morning of the ninth day, probing through the smoke hole with his stick and finding no snow to push away, Jim Clyman took the shovel that he had brought in from the wagon, and began to dig. The snow, eight feet of which had fallen in eight days, was almost even with the top of the rude shelter. Working the point of his shovel up along the side of the door, he pushed the snow aside, and blinked in the unaccustomed flood of light. He continued to dig, enlarging the hole. Then, cutting steps as he went, he dug upward and outward, and emerged into a white, silent world. To one side, the shelter in which Cressman had crouched alone for eight days was only a soft mound on top of the snow blanket.

Jim Clyman slipped his feet into the harnesses of the homemade snowshoes and walked over to Cressman's shelter. He shoveled a hole down to the door, shouted, and when muffled sounds emerged, dropped the shovel down. Cressman had survived, and could dig himself out.

Young Nate Parker, who had come out of the shelter to try his first experimental steps on snowshoes, floundered over. "Say, is this snow deep!" he panted.

The little brown dog frisked happily about, his big paws better support on the crystalline crust than the snowshoes of the heavier human beings. The mountain man watched thoughtfully, his lips pursed. A dog was really something to have when a man was out this way. The least you could say about him was that he never worried. But then, neither did young 'uns—all Nate Parker could think of was the wonderful depth of the snow. But he could take care of himself. Ann couldn't, and it was going to be a mite of a problem to get the little tyke over the divide and down the other slope.

He reached over to slash a thong that bore a twenty-pound chunk of horse meat aloft on a pine branch, and caught it in his hands as it fell.

"Take this inside, will you, Nate?" he called.

The boy carried the frozen chunk of meat into the tepee, and a moment later his uncle and aunt came out. They glanced at the shelter where Cressman had cleared a hole for himself and was working to shovel his way to the top of the snow, then set to work helping to carry the rest of the meat into their shelter. With the ax, Clyman began chopping the frozen stuff into thin slices, then used his knife to pare the rest of it from the bones. He had begun to make up four packs when Cressman came down into the shelter and stood sullenly watching him.

"Where's the fifth one?" Cressman demanded.

Jim Clyman said reasonably, "I figger we men can pack mebbe thirty-five pounds each up the slope. Nate's takin' twenty-five."

"What about her?"

"The little girl can't wear snowshoes, so somebody's got to help her all the time, and carry her some of the time. We'll take turns."

Cressman sputtered belligerently. "You know we ain't got much chance of gettin' out of here unless we haul every ounce of food we can!"

"We're takin' four packs." Clyman's voice was smooth. "I told you before I'm big buck at this lick."

Cressman subsided, and Jim Clyman went on making up the packs. He folded a portion of the meat in a square torn from the wagon cover, and formed broad shoulder straps with more of the same material. A blanket was tied to each pack, and two to his own. The little remaining flour he wrapped in a strip of buckskin and put in his own pack. Finally he hung his powder horn at his belt and put half a dozen bullets in his pocket. One rifle was enough. More would be extra weight. He rose.

"Cressman, you carry the ax."

"I'll carry it," Nate Parker offered.

"Cressman will."

He climbed up the steps he had chopped and stood for a moment in the snow on top of them. The little dog crowded close to his heels and squatted down on the tails of his snowshoes while he waited for the rest to join him. They started west toward the slope, Kate Parker and Ann behind Clyman, then Cressman, with George and Nate Parker bringing up the rear. Jim Clyman walked a quarter of a mile and turned around. Kate Paker smiled at him. But there was sweat on her face and she was breathing heavily.

The mountain man went on without slowing his pace. It was a right long way over the pass and down the opposite slope, and they'd better push it hard while they were well-fed and rested. When, and if, they got out of these mountains, they might be crawling on their hands and knees. He studied the clouds that hung low over the mountain peaks, and pushed on another mile before stopping. Then he waited for Kate Parker to close the gap that had imperceptibly widened between them. She was now carrying Ann.

"That little mite you got there," he said, "could rest easy as nothin' on top of my own pack for a spell."

"I'll carry her, Mr. Clyman," the mother said with quiet dignity.

Clyman turned and went on. Immigrants bound for California might be senseless folks who hadn't the least idea of how to take care of themselves. But there was no denying that some of them possessed courage of a sort to brighten the eye of the doughtiest[3] mountain man. Kate Parker's baby was going over the divide with her. She might have to pant to hold up her end. But her baby was still going with her.

* * *

The next day they struck the steepest part of the slope and began to claw and fight their way up it. Storm clouds milled angrily above them, and it was bitingly cold. Jim Clyman stopped to turn and look back through the half-gloom, and his brown dog gladly sat down in the tracks he had made. One by one the rest struggled up and stood panting near him. The mountain man measured with his eye the distance to the top of the divide, and anxiously studied the clouds. A rising gust of wind blew a whirling line of snow around them. Not seeming to hurry, but still moving purposefully, Jim Clyman paused behind each pack-laden man and cut the blanket from his back. He spread two of them on the snow.

"We ain't goin' to make it," he said in a matter-of-fact voice. "Sit in a circle on these blankets, and I'll put the others over us. Every person's responsible for holdin' down his part. The baby goes in the middle. We ain't gonna freeze if we do it right. It's an old mountain man's trick."

They sat down on the blankets obediently enough. Clyman pulled the rest over them, tucking them in closely. He closed the last gap with his own body as the storm began to rage down in full fury. Dry snow piled on top of the improvised tent. The little dog whimpered in the darkness, and the child talked baby gibberish. All that night, nibbling at

---

3 **doughtiest:** most fearless

the pemmican that they carried, they crouched under the blankets and kept each other warm with body heat. Then they pushed the snow from the blankets, and rising like specters,[4] floundered on their way through the soft snow.

That day they got over the divide. Jim Clyman stood at the top of it, waiting for the rest to straggle up. First Cressman came. Then Nathan Parker appeared, and finally George and Kate Parker appeared, the

RESCUE IN THE SNOW
1906
N.C. Wyeth

4 **specter:** *ghost*

father carrying Ann. The mountain man stared at them silently. Coming up that murderous, snow-filled slope, George Parker had thrown his food pack away to help his wife and baby. Jim Clyman could not find the heart to reproach him. He turned to start down the slope.

"I was wrong about him, Bub," he muttered to the tired little dog. "He *can* make up his own mind."

* * *

Two days later Jim Clyman turned off the trail into the forest. With the ax that he had taken from Cressman he chopped down four small trees. He trimmed the branches from them, and cut the trunks in half. Then he arranged the logs on the ten feet of snow that lay there, made a little pile of shaven pitch-pine sticks, and poured a pinch of powder from his powder horn. He struck up a spark into the powder, and the fire flared up. The little brown dog lay near the comforting warmth, paws outspread and tongue lolling expectantly as he glanced up at his master.

The mountain man looked back up the irregular line of snowshoe tracks he had made coming down, and frowned. He and the dog could have been another fifteen miles down the slope by this time. But you couldn't travel that way with tenderfeet. Not that anyone except Cressman had hung back, or complained of cold and hunger. They just weren't making it so well. George Parker and his wife were taking turns carrying the little girl, but they had to rest every little while. Nate, the boy, had plodded steadily along with his lightening pack—and it had been lightened because Jim Clyman insisted on using the food he carried before any other. Now that was gone, and Parker's was gone. He would start using Cressman's tonight, and save his own for the last hard stretch. He had rationed the food carefully, and they should make it if the tenderfeet could keep up and if another bad blizzard didn't hit them.

As he threw more wood on the fire, the dog rose from his bed in the snow and cocked his head up the trail. Nathan Parker appeared, stumbling down the snowshoe tracks with his head bent and his eyes streaming. The sun had shone brightly all day, and the Parkers and Cressman couldn't seem to get the knack of avoiding snow blindness by squinting properly. But there was no point in exaggerating burdens, or stressing them.

"Doggonit, Nate," he said. "I thought you'd took off on another track."

"Nope." The boy gave a tired grin and sat down to slip the blanket from his shoulders. "I'll stick."

"Reckon you will. Well, fire's ready. Where's the others?"

"They're comin'."

Kate and George Parker, with the little girl riding on her father's shoulders, staggered along the trail and threw themselves wearily down by the leaping fire. Tired as she was, the mother took the child and cradled her in her arms. Jim Clyman petted his dog, and watched them reflectively. Once a mountain man had come stumbling into his camp. He had traveled almost seven hundred miles through hostile country, he said, and for the past nine days he had had nothing to eat. Many times he had been tempted to give up and die, but he had kept himself alive by thinking of the buffalo steak he was going to have as soon as he got into somebody's camp. That man had lived on hope. Hope was a wonderful thing, a sustaining resource when all others failed. The Parkers had it in large measure.

Cressman came in to the fire and sat with his head hunched over his chest, staring with vacant eyes at the flames. Clyman looked keenly at him. Cressman, the laggard, who had been hanging back more than anyone else the past three days, seemed more fit and ready to go on than any of the others. His face was fuller; his color better. But his expression was becoming more beast than human. The old man's eyes narrowed.

"Let's have your pack, Cressman. Time for grub—such as it is."

"My pack? *My* pack . . . ?"

Cressman raised his head, and glanced crookedly about. He dropped the pack, and the mountain man stepped forward to unfasten the thongs that bound it. But even before he did he knew that it was empty. He took a step forward, his knife in his hand. A deep anger leaped within him, and red shapes wavered before his eyes.

"You ate it!" he snarled. "You ate it, didn't you? That's why you hung back!"

The hot cloud of rage slowly dissolved, and he again became leader of the little group. Dimly he saw the rest looking at Cressman, saw civilized eyes glowing red in the reflection of the fire, betraying a deep, elemental passion that went far, far back. They were primitive people, cave people who had seen their food stolen. Cressman did not notice them. His eyes were rolling, a vacuous grin played about his lips. The trail was driving him mad.

"Eat the dog," he babbled. "We c'n eat the dog."

Jim Clyman stuck his knife in a log, drew his pack to him, and pulled out a small piece of frozen meat. He saw the eager eyes of the Parkers fixed upon him now, the greedy eyes of the half-mad Cressman. Cressman started to rise, his hands twitching. Clyman reached for his knife.

"Sit down!" he growled. "Mebbe you eat tomorrow, but not tonight. You've had your'n!"

He had cut two thin slices of meat for each of the others, impaled them on sticks, and put them over the fire to cook. Melting snow in the kettle, he stirred a little flour into it, flavored with a tiny piece of meat, and handed it to Kate Parker. The baby ate hungrily, but when the mother was given her own ration, she shook her head.

"Can't I save it for tomorrow?"

Beneath her question was a deeper and more penetrating one. There was tomorrow, and the next day, and the next . . . . The baby had to eat all those days. The future generation must survive.

"Eat it now," Jim Clyman said gruffly.

She did, tearing the meat into tiny morsels with her teeth and devouring them reluctantly. While they ate, Clyman never took his eyes from Cressman. But the man was apathetic, mumbling to himself and smiling foolishly. When they had finished, the mountain man spoke as cheerfully as he could.

"I been in such fixes before, and I'll be in 'em ag'in. We're gonna get through. But if anybody touches my pack, I'll kill him."

"Eat the dog," Cressman raved. "Kill and eat the dog."

Clyman glanced across the fire at him, and said nothing. But when he rolled up in his blanket that night, the dog was beside him.

* * *

Jim Clyman himself was not exactly sure as to what took place the next few days. He knew only that the two slices of meat were cut to one, and that when they finally came out of the deep snow they cut the lacings from their snowshoes, boiled them, and drank the gelatinous soup. The last of the meat he carried had been eaten yesterday morning, while starved eyes had looked at the little brown dog and then guiltily away again. This morning the baby had had the last of the flour.

He walked on, the spaniel dragging wearily at his heels. On either side the tall pines rustled, and the racing little brook he was following cast itself furiously over the ice-sheathed rocks and boulders in its path. It seemed that he was back at the time when the starved hunter had wandered into camp. That memory was very plain and very sharp. The hunter, he remembered, had lived entirely on hope, on the hope of a meal of buffalo meat. But tenderfeet weren't mountain men. They wouldn't believe that they were going to get anything unless they could see it before them. And all they could see was his dog. . . .

He forced himself back to reality. Behind him were people, hungry people, each of whom, in his own way, thought of the things nearest and dearest to him. Cressman, in his insane wanderings, had gone back to his farm on the Fox River and was enjoying all the things it had once offered him. Nathan Parker thought of going on, of continuing to follow this man who had dared suggest coming over the divide when it was impassable. George and Kate Parker thought of the child in her arms, and of all the life that was to be.

But their whole minds, when they were at either the morning or the evening fire, centered on the little brown dog and the salvation he offered. Here was food, and food was life, and they had to live. They could not be lured this far, then die within reach of their goal. He turned aside and gathered wood for a fire. He poured a little gunpowder under the wood and lighted it. Tonight they would camp out of the winter snow. The little dog lay down before the fire with his head on his paws.

Nathan Parker appeared, and almost as soon as he sat down beside the fire his eyes fastened on the dog. Carrying the little girl between them, Kate and George Parker came stumbling out of the semi-gloom. Cressman crawled up, babbling of fat sheep that had grazed beside the Fox River and of the many meals he had eaten there. Then he, too, fell silent, and all eyes were fixed on the dog.

Jim Clayman edged his knife out of its sheath. An animal was not supposed to mean anything when human lives were at stake, but the little spaniel was more to him than any person. He was a friend, one to whom he could confide his innermost thoughts and troubles, one who had always been satisfied to share his fortune. The knife point stopped at the dog's throat, and Clyman held it there while he looked at the eager people about the fire. They had been led on by tangible hope, by certain knowledge that, when their last food gave out, they had a final resource in the dog. And they could go no farther without food. The dog would feed them tonight, tomorrow, and perhaps the day after. It would see them through. He touched the knife against the dog's throat, and the spaniel whimpered in his arms.

"Well, by God!"

It was not a curse but a prayer, and it came from outside the circle of firelight. A tall man with a rifle in his hands stood there, a strong, well-fed man with a pack on his back.

"You came over the divide?" he asked incredulously.

They struggled to their feet, staring in disbelief at this man who had brought them salvation. The caveman had gone from them. They were once again civilized, thinking people.

"Got caught out on a long survey," the stranger explained, "and saw your fire. Our camp's only a piece down the trail, but I reckon you'd better eat right here." He swung his pack to the ground.

Jim Clyman slowly slipped his knife back in its sheath, and tickled the little dog's ears with a bony finger. "We made it, Bub," he said huskily. "We made it. This here's the end of the trail." ⁌

RESPONDING TO CLUSTER TWO

WHAT WERE THE EFFECTS OF MANIFEST DESTINY?

THINKING SKILL   COMPARING AND CONTRASTING

1. The essay "Touching the Skirts of Heaven" describes the physical hardships and emotional isolation of the early pioneers. Which would you find more difficult to endure? Explain your answer.

2. List at least four reasons explorers and pioneers had for traveling to the frontier. Think of some practical as well as idealistic reasons for leaving home.

3. Using what you have learned from this book and elsewhere, complete the chart below to **analyze** the effects of Manifest Destiny on the following:

	Before	After
Pioneers		
Native Americans		
North American ecosystem		

4. Do you believe Manifest Destiny was a valid policy? Explain why or why not.

5. **Compare** the fictional "End of the Trail" with the oral history "Tsali of the Cherokees." In your opinion, which piece more powerfully conveys the effects of Manifest Destiny on ordinary people? Why?

Writing Activity: A Pioneer Woman's Diary

Imagine you are one of the female characters in any of the selections in Cluster Two. In your journal, **compare** and **contrast** your life on the frontier to the sort of life you left behind. You can also **compare** and **contrast** your life with the men's. What are some of your struggles? Your pleasures? Be precise with physical details, emotions, and reactions to the new landscape and experiences.

Writing a Journal

• include the date and the place you are writing from.

• use only language that would be familiar to people in the 1800s.

• include specific details that will add up to the portrait of a particular person and her experience of the frontier.

CLUSTER THREE

Who Were the People of the Frontier?

Thinking Skill SUMMARIZING

Jim Bridger (1804–1881) frontiersman, trapper, and scout

GOLD RUSH!

Swiss immigrant John Augustus Sutter lived a comfortable life on his 50,000-acre estate in northern California. On January 24, 1848, his life changed when mill foreman James Marshall brought several shiny rocks to Sutter. They tried to keep the discovery of gold a secret, but soon the ranch was overrun with hundreds of thousands of "Forty-Niners" hoping to strike it rich. Sutter was bankrupted by claim jumpers—thieves who would file claims on land already owned by another— and hungry miners who stole his livestock.

A prospector pans for gold

Californian

March 15, 1848

GOLD MINE FOUND

—In the newly made raceway of the Saw Mill recently erected by Captain Sutter, on the American Fork, gold has been found in considerable quantities. One person brought thirty dollars worth to New Helvetia, gathered there in a short time. California, no doubt, is rich in mineral wealth; great chances here for scientific capitalists. Gold has been found in almost every part of the country.

The Hartford Daily Courant

Wednesday Morning, December 6, 1848

THE GOLD FEVER

The California gold fever is approaching its crisis. We are told that the new region that has just become a part of our possessions, is El Dorado after all.—Thither is now setting a tide that will not cease its flow until either untold wealth is amassed, or extended beggary is secured. By a sudden and accidental discovery, the ground is represented to be one vast gold mine.—Gold is picked up in pure lumps, twenty-four carats fine. Soldiers are deserting their ranks, sailors their ships, and every body their employment, to speed to the region of the gold mines. In a moment, as it were, a desert country, that never deserved much notice from the world, has become the centre of universal attraction. Every body, by the accounts, is getting money at a rate that puts all past experience in that line far in the shade. The stories are evidently thickening in interest, as do the arithmetical calculations connected with them in importance. Fifteen millions have already come into the possession of somebody, and all creation is going out there to fill their pockets with the great condiment of their diseased minds.

Levi's

Jacob W. Davis

Jacob W. Davis, a tailor in Reno, Nevada, created a new type of pants using rivets to secure the pockets and seams. But his wife said he couldn't spend money on another patent. So Davis wrote to his fabric supplier Levi Strauss in San Francisco. Levi Strauss & Co was a large dry goods store with traveling salesmen who sold to miners at the diggings. Davis might have been literate in Yiddish, but he dictated this letter to a pharmacist who translated it into English.

Cowboys wear 'levis'
for the hard, dirty
work of branding
cattle, 1888

July 2, 1872
San Francisco

I also send you by Express 2 ps. Overall as you will
see one Blue and one made of the 10 oz Duck which
I have bought in greate many Peces of you, and have
made it up in to Pents, such as the sample.

The secratt of them Pents is the Rivits that I put in
those Pockets and I found the demand so large that I
cannot make them up fast enough. I charge for the Duck
$3.00 and the Blue $2.50 a pear. My nabors are getting
yealouse of these success and unless I secure it by Patent
Papers it will soon become a general thing. Everybody will
make them up and thare will be no money in it.

Therefore Gentleman, I wish to make you a Proposition
that you should take out the Latters Patent in my
name as I am the inventor of it, the expense of it will
be about $68, all complit and for these $68 will give
you half the right to sell all such clothing Revited
according to the Patent, for all the Pacific States and
Teroterious, the balince of the United States and half of
the Pacific Coast I resarve for myself. The investment
for you is but a trifle compaired with the improvement
in all Coarse Clothing. I use it in all Blankit Clothing
such as Coats, Vests and Pents, and you will find it a
very salable article at a much advenst rate. . . .

These looks like a trifle hardley worth speaking off but
nevertheless I knew you can make a very large amount
of money on it. If you make up Pents the way I do you
can sell Duck Pents such as the Sample at $30. per doz.
and they will readly retail for $3. a pair.

Jacob W. Davis

BOOMERS AND SOONERS:
THE GREAT LAND RUSH

William W. Howard

Oklahoma was Indian Territory—several tribes had been removed from the Southeast and settled there after the forced march known as the Trail of Tears. Thousands of freed slaves also fled to Oklahoma after the Civil War to avoid whites.

But white homesteaders encroached even in Indian Territory. In 1889, the government opened the territory for white settlement. The land was given away free to the 60,000 eager Boomers who waited for the pistol shot that announced the final frontier was open for settlement. "Sooners" snuck onto the land early and staked their claims, popping up only after they had seen the first settlers approach.

Eyewitness William W. Howard wrote this account for Harper's Weekly.

Guthrie, Oklahoma, April 22, 1889

Unlike Rome the city of Guthrie was built in a day. To be strictly accurate in the matter, it might be said that it was built in an afternoon. At twelve o'clock on Monday, April 22d, the resident population of Guthrie was nothing; before sundown it was at least ten thousand. In that time streets had been laid out, town lots staked off, and steps taken toward the formation of a municipal government. At twilight the campfires of ten thousand people gleamed on the grassy slopes of the Cimarron Valley, where, the night before, the coyote, the gray wolf, and the deer

The wait [inset] and the mad dash
into Oklahoma to claim free land,
April 22, 1889

EYEWITNESS ACCOUNT   95

had roamed undisturbed. Never before in the history of the West has so large a number of people been concentrated in one place in so short a time. To the conservative Eastern man, who is wont to see cities grow by decades, the settlement of Guthrie was magical beyond belief, to the quick-acting resident of the West, it was merely a particularly lively townsite speculation.

The preparations for the settlement of Oklahoma had been complete, even to the slightest detail, for weeks before the opening day. The Santa Fe Railway, which runs through Oklahoma north and south, was prepared to take any number of people from its handsome station at Arkansas City, Kansas, and to deposit them in almost any part of Oklahoma as soon as the law allowed; thousands of covered wagons were gathered in camps on all sides of the new Territory waiting for the embargo to be lifted.

In its picturesque aspects the rush across the border at noon on the opening day must go down in history as one of the most noteworthy events of Western civilization. At the time fixed, thousands of hungry home-seekers, who had gathered from all parts of the country, and particularly from Kansas and Missouri, were arranged in line along the border, ready to lash their horses into furious speed in the race for fertile spots in the beautiful land before them.

As the expectant home-seekers waited with restless patience, the clear, sweet notes of a cavalry bugle rose and hung a moment upon the startled air. It was noon. The last barrier of savagery in the United States was broken down.

Moved by the same impulse, each driver lashed his horses furiously; each rider dug his spurs into his willing steed, and each man on foot caught his breath hard and darted forward.

A cloud of dust rose where the home-seekers had stood in line, and when it had drifted away before the gentle breeze, the horses and wagons and men were tearing across the open country like fiends.

The horsemen had the best of it from the start. It was a fine race for a few minutes, but soon the riders began to spread out like a fan, and by the time they had reached the horizon they were scattered about as far as eye could see. Even the fleetest of the horsemen found upon reaching their chosen localities that men in wagons and men on foot were there before them.

As it was clearly impossible for a man on foot to outrun a horseman, the inference is plain that Oklahoma had been entered hours before the appointed time. Notwithstanding the assertions of the soldiers that every boomer had been driven out of Oklahoma, the fact remains that the woods along the various streams within Oklahoma were literally full of people Sunday night.

Nine-tenths of these people made settlement upon the land illegally. The other tenth would have done so had there been any desirable land left to settle upon. This action on the part of the first claim-holders will cause a great deal of land litigation in the future, as it is not to be expected that the man who ran his horse at its utmost speed for ten miles only to find a settler with an ox team in quiet possession of his chosen farm will tamely submit to this plain infringement of the law.

Some of the men who started from the line on foot were quite as successful in securing desirable claims as many who rode fleet horses. They had the advantage of knowing just where their land was located. One man left the line with the others, carrying on his back a tent, a blanket, some camp dishes, an ax, and provisions for two days. He ran down the railway track for six miles, and reached his claim in just sixty minutes. Upon arriving on his land he fell down under a tree, unable to speak or see. I am glad to be able to say that his claim is one of the best in Oklahoma.

The rush from the line was so impetuous that when the first railway train arrived from the north at twenty-five minutes past twelve o'clock, only a few of the hundreds of boomers were anywhere to be seen.

The journey of this first train was well-nigh as interesting as the rush of the men in wagons. The train left Arkansas City at 8:45 o'clock in the forenoon. It consisted of an empty baggage car, which was set apart for the use of the newspaper correspondents, eight passenger coaches, and the caboose of a freight train. The coaches were so densely packed with men that not another human being could get on board. So uncomfortably crowded were they that some of the younger boomers climbed to the roofs of the cars and clung perilously to the ventilators. An adventurous person secured at great risk a seat on the forward truck of the baggage car.

Hardly had the train slackened its speed when the impatient boomers began to leap from the cars and run up the slope. Men jumped from the roofs of the moving cars at the risk of their lives. Some were so stunned by the fall that they could not get up for some minutes. The coaches were so crowded that many men were compelled to squeeze through the windows in order to get a fair start at the head of the crowd. Almost before the train had come to a standstill the cars were emptied.

In their haste and eagerness, men fell over each other in heaps, others stumbled and fell headlong, while many ran forward so blindly and impetuously that it was not until they had passed the best of the town lots that they came to a realization of their actions.

It is estimated that between six and seven thousand persons reached Guthrie by train from the north the first afternoon, and that fully three thousand came in by wagon from the north and east, and by train from Purcell on the south, thus making a total population for the first day of about ten thousand.

By taking thought in the matter, three-fourths of these people had provided themselves with tents and blankets, so that even on the first night they had ample shelter from the weather. The rest of them slept the first night as best they could, with only the red earth for a pillow and the starry arch of heaven for a blanket.

At dawn of Tuesday the unrefreshed home-seekers and town-site speculators arose, and began anew the location of disputed claims. The tents multiplied like mushrooms in a rain that day, and by night the building of frame houses had been begun in earnest in the new streets. The buildings were by no means elaborate, yet they were as good as the average frontier structure, and they served their purpose, which was all that was required.

On that day the trains going north were filled with returning boomers, disgusted beyond expression with the dismal outlook of the new country. Their places were taken by others who came in to see the fun, and perhaps pick up a bargain in the way of town lots or commercial speculation.

During the first three days food was nearly as hard to get as water. Dusty ham sandwiches sold on the streets as high as twenty-five cents each, while in the restaurants a plate of pork and beans was valued at seventy-five cents. Few men were well enough provided with funds to buy themselves a hearty meal. One disgusted home-seeker estimated that if he ate as much as he was accustomed to eat back in Missouri his board would cost him $7.75 per day. Not being able to spend that amount of money every day, he contented himself with such stray sandwiches as were within his means. In this manner he contrived to subsist until Wednesday afternoon, when he was forced to return to civilization in southern Kansas in order to keep from starving to death.

A year after the Oklahoma land rush, the federal census showed the physical frontier no longer existed. The population stretched from coast to coast.

Tent towns sprang up overnight during the Oklahoma land rush.

THE BRIDE COMES TO YELLOW SKY

Stephen Crane

I

The great Pullman was whirling onward with such dignity of motion that a glance from the window seemed simply to prove that the plains of Texas were pouring eastward. Vast flats of green grass, dull-hued spaces of mesquite and cactus, little groups of frame houses, woods of light and tender trees, all were sweeping into the east, sweeping over the horizon, a precipice.

A newly married pair had boarded this coach at San Antonio. The man's face was reddened from many days in the wind and sun, and a direct result of his new black clothes was that his brick-colored hands were constantly performing in a most conscious fashion. From time to time he looked down respectfully at his attire. He sat with a hand on each knee, like a man waiting in a barber's shop. The glances he devoted to other passengers were furtive and shy.

The bride was not pretty, nor was she very young. She wore a dress of blue cashmere, with small reservations of velvet here and there, and with steel buttons abounding. She continually twisted her head to regard her puff sleeves, very stiff, straight, and high. They embarrassed her. It was quite apparent that she had cooked, and that she expected to cook, dutifully. The blushes caused by the careless scrutiny of some passengers as she had entered the car were strange to see upon this plain, underclass countenance, which was drawn in placid, almost emotionless lines.

They were evidently very happy. "Ever been in a parlor car before?" he asked, smiling with delight.

"No," she answered. "I never was. It's fine, ain't it?"

"Great! And then after a while we'll go forward to the diner, and get a big layout. Finest meal in the world. Charge a dollar."

"Oh, do they?" cried the bride. "Charge a dollar? Why, that's too much—for us—ain't it, Jack?"

"Not this trip, anyhow," he answered bravely. "We're going to go the whole thing."

Later, he explained to her about the trains. "You see, it's a thousand miles from one end of Texas to the other; and this train runs right across it, and never stops but four times." He had the pride of an owner. He pointed out to her the dazzling fittings of the coach; and in truth her eyes opened wider as she contemplated the sea-green figured velvet, the shining brass, silver, and glass, the wood that gleamed as darkly brilliant as the surface of a pool of oil. At one end a bronze figure sturdily held a support for a separated chamber, and at convenient places on the ceiling were frescoes in olive and silver.

To the minds of the pair, their surroundings reflected the glory of their marriage that morning in San Antonio. This was the environment of their new estate, and the man's face in particular beamed with an elation that made him appear ridiculous to the negro porter. This individual at times surveyed them from afar with an amused and superior grin. On other occasions he bullied them with skill in ways that did not make it exactly plain to them that they were being bullied. He subtly used all the manners of the most unconquerable kind of snobbery. He oppressed them; but of this oppression they had small knowledge, and they speedily forgot that infrequently a number of travelers covered them with stares of derisive enjoyment. Historically there was supposed to be something infinitely humorous in their situation.

"We are due in Yellow Sky at 3:42," he said, looking tenderly into her eyes.

"Oh, are we?" she said, as if she had not been aware of it. To evince surprise at her husband's statement was part of her wifely amiability. She took from a pocket a little silver watch, and as she held it before her, and stared at it with a frown of attention, the new husband's face shone.

"I bought it in San Anton' from a friend of mine," he told her gleefully.

"It's seventeen minutes past twelve," she said, looking up at him with a kind of shy and clumsy coquetry. A passenger, noting this play, grew excessively sardonic, and winked at himself in one of the numerous mirrors.

At last they went to the dining car. Two rows of negro waiters, in glowing white suits, surveyed their entrance with the interest, and also the equanimity, of men who had been forewarned. The pair fell to the lot of a waiter who happened to feel pleasure in steering them through their meal. He viewed them with the manner of a fatherly pilot, his countenance radiant with benevolence. The patronage, entwined with the ordinary deference, was not plain to them. And yet, as they returned to their coach, they showed in their faces a sense of escape.

To the left, miles down a long purple slope, was a little ribbon of mist where moved the keening Rio Grande. The train was approaching it at an angle, and the apex was Yellow Sky. Presently it was apparent that, as the distance from Yellow Sky grew shorter, the husband became commensurately restless. His brick-red hands were more insistent in their prominence. Occasionally he was even rather absent-minded and faraway when the bride leaned forward and addressed him.

As a matter of truth, Jack Potter was beginning to find the shadow of a deed weigh upon him like a leaden slab. He, the town marshal of Yellow Sky, a man known, liked, and feared in his corner, a prominent person, had gone to San Antonio to meet a girl he believed he loved, and there, after the usual prayers, had actually induced her to marry him, without consulting Yellow Sky for any part of the transaction. He was now bringing his bride before an innocent and unsuspecting community.

Of course, people in Yellow Sky married as it pleased them, in accordance with a general custom; but such was Potter's thought of his duty to his friends, or of their idea of his duty, or of an unspoken form which does not control men in these matters, that he felt he was heinous. He had committed an extraordinary crime. Face to face with this girl in San Antonio, and spurred by his sharp impulse, he had gone headlong over all the social hedges. At San Antonio he was like a man hidden in the dark. A knife to sever any friendly duty, any form, was easy to his hand in that remote city. But the hour of Yellow Sky—the hour of daylight—was approaching.

He knew full well that his marriage was an important thing to his town. It could only be exceeded by the burning of the new hotel. His friends could not forgive him. Frequently he had reflected on the advisability of telling them by telegraph, but a new cowardice had been upon him. He feared to do it. And now the train was hurrying him toward a scene of amazement, glee, and reproach. He glanced out of the window at the line of haze swinging slowly in toward the train.

Yellow Sky had a kind of brass band, which played painfully, to the delight of the populace. He laughed without heart as he thought of it. If the citizens could dream of his prospective arrival with his bride, they would parade the band at the station and escort them, amid cheers and laughing congratulations, to his adobe home.

He resolved that he would use all the devices of speed and plainscraft in making the journey from the station to his house. Once within that safe citadel, he could issue some sort of a vocal bulletin, and then not go among the citizens until they had time to wear off a little of their enthusiasm.

The bride looked anxiously at him. "What's worrying you, Jack?"

He laughed again. "I'm not worrying, girl. I'm only thinking of Yellow Sky."

She flushed in comprehension.

A sense of mutual guilt invaded their minds and developed a finer tenderness. They looked at each other with eyes softly aglow. But Potter often laughed the same nervous laugh. The flush upon the bride's face seemed quite permanent.

The traitor to the feelings of Yellow Sky narrowly watched the speeding landscape. "We're nearly there," he said.

Presently the porter came and announced the proximity of Potter's home. He held a brush in his hand, and, with all his airy superiority gone, he brushed Potter's new clothes as the latter slowly turned this way and that way. Potter fumbled out a coin and gave it to the porter, as he had seen others do. It was a heavy and muscle-bound business, as that of a man shoeing his first horse.

The porter took their bag, and as the train began to slow they moved forward to the hooded platform of the car. Presently the two engines and their long string of coaches rushed into the station of Yellow Sky.

"They have to take water here," said Potter, from a constricted throat and in mournful cadence, as one announcing death. Before the train stopped, his eye had swept the length of the platform, and he was glad and astonished to see there was none upon it but the station-agent, who, with a slightly hurried and anxious air, was walking toward the water tanks. When the train had halted, the porter alighted first and placed in position a little temporary step.

"Come on, girl," said Potter, hoarsely. As he helped her down they each laughed on a false note. He took the bag from the negro, and bade his wife cling to his arm. As they slunk rapidly away, his hangdog glance perceived that they were unloading the two trunks, and also that the station-agent, far ahead near the baggage car, had turned and was running toward him, making gestures. He laughed, and groaned as he laughed, when he noted the first effect of his marital bliss upon Yellow Sky. He gripped his wife's arm firmly to his side, and they fled. Behind them the porter stood, chuckling fatuously.

II

The California express on the Southern Railway was due at Yellow Sky in twenty-one minutes. There were six men at the bar of the "Weary Gentleman" saloon. One was a drummer[1] who talked a great deal and rapidly; three were Texans who did not care to talk at that time; and two were Mexican sheepherders who did not talk as a general practice in the Weary Gentleman saloon. The barkeeper's dog lay on the board-walk that crossed in front of the door. His head was on his paws, and he glanced drowsily here and there with the constant vigilance of a dog

---

1 **drummer:** traveling salesman

that is kicked on occasion. Across the sandy street were some vivid green grass-plots, so wonderful in appearance amid the sands that burned near them in a blazing sun that they caused a doubt in the mind. They exactly resembled the grass mats used to represent lawns on the stage. At the cooler end of the railway station, a man without a coat sat in a tilted chair and smoked his pipe. The fresh-cut bank of the Rio Grande circled near the town, and there could be seen beyond it a great plum-colored plain of mesquite.

Save for the busy drummer and his companions in the saloon, Yellow Sky was dozing. The newcomer leaned gracefully upon the bar, and recited many tales with the confidence of a bard who has come upon a new field.

"—and at the moment that the old man fell downstairs with the bureau in his arms, the old woman was coming up with two scuttles of coal, and of course—"

The drummer's tale was interrupted by a young man who suddenly appeared in the open door. He cried: "Scratchy Wilson's drunk, and has turned loose with both hands." The two Mexicans at once set down their glasses and faded out of the rear entrance of the saloon.

The drummer, innocent and jocular, answered: "All right, old man. S'pose he has? Come in and have a drink, anyhow."

But the information had made such an obvious cleft in every skull in the room that the drummer was obliged to see its importance. All had become instantly solemn. "Say," said he, mystified, "what is this?" His three companions made the introductory gesture of eloquent speech, but the young man at the door forestalled them.

"It means, my friend," he answered, as he came into the saloon, "that for the next two hours this town won't be a health resort."

The barkeeper went to the door and locked and barred it. Reaching out of the window, he pulled in heavy wooden shutters and barred them. Immediately a solemn, chapel-like gloom was upon the place. The drummer was looking from one to another.

"But say," he cried, "what is this, anyhow? You don't mean there is going to be a gunfight?"

"Don't know whether there'll be a fight or not," answered one man, grimly. "But there'll be some shootin'—some good shootin'."

The young man who had warned them waved his hand. "Oh, there'll be a fight fast enough, if any one wants it. Anybody can get a fight out there in the street. There's a fight just waiting."

The drummer seemed to be swayed between the interest of a foreigner and a perception of personal danger.

"What did you say his name was?" he asked.

"Scratchy Wilson," they answered in chorus.

"And will he kill anybody? What are you going to do? Does this happen often? Does he rampage around like this once a week or so? Can he break in that door?"

"No; he can't break down that door," replied the barkeeper. "He's tried it three times. But when he comes you'd better lay down on the floor, stranger. He's dead sure to shoot at it, and a bullet may come through."

Thereafter the drummer kept a strict eye upon the door. The time had not yet been called for him to hug the floor, but, as a minor precaution, he sidled near to the wall. "Will he kill anybody?" he said again.

The men laughed low and scornfully at the question.

"He's out to shoot, and he's out for trouble. Don't see any good in experimentin' with him."

"But what do you do in a case like this? What do you do?"

A man responded: "Why, he and Jack Potter—"

"But," in chorus the other men interrupted, "Jack Potter's in San Anton'."

"Well, who is he? What's he got to do with it?"

"Oh, he's the town marshal. He goes out and fights Scratchy when he gets on one of these tears."

"Wow!" said the drummer, mopping his brow. "Nice job he's got."

The voices had toned away to mere whisperings. The drummer wished to ask further questions, which were born of an increasing anxiety and bewilderment; but when he attempted them, the men merely looked at him in irritation and motioned him to remain silent. A tense waiting hush was upon them. In the deep shadows of the room their eyes shone as they listened for sounds from the street. One man made three gestures at the barkeeper; and the latter, moving like a ghost, handed him a glass and a bottle. The man poured a full glass of whisky, and set down the bottle noiselessly. He gulped the whisky in a swallow, and turned again toward the door in immovable silence. The drummer saw that the barkeeper, without a sound, had taken a Winchester from beneath the bar. Later he saw this individual beckoning to him, so he tiptoed across the room.

"You better come with me back of the bar."

"No, thanks," said the drummer, perspiring. "I'd rather be where I can make a break for the back door."

Whereupon the man of bottles made a kindly but peremptory gesture. The drummer obeyed it, and, finding himself seated on a box with his head below the level of the bar, balm was laid upon his soul at sight of various zinc and copper fittings that bore a resemblance to armor plate. The barkeeper took a seat comfortably upon an adjacent box.

"You see," he whispered, "this here Scratchy Wilson is a wonder with a gun—a perfect wonder—and when he goes on the war trail, we hunt our holes—naturally. He's about the last one of the old gang that used to hang out along the river here. He's a terror when he's drunk. When he's sober he's all right—kind of simple—wouldn't hurt a fly—nicest fellow in town. But when he's drunk—whoo!"

There were periods of stillness. "I wish Jack Potter was back from San Anton'," said the barkeeper. "He shot Wilson up once—in the leg—and he would sail in and pull out the kinks in this thing."

Presently they heard from a distance the sound of a shot, followed by three wild yowls. It instantly removed a bond from the men in the darkened saloon. There was a shuffling of feet. They looked at each other. "Here he comes," they said.

III

A man in a maroon-colored flannel shirt, which had been purchased for purposes of decoration, and made principally by some Jewish women on the East Side of New York, rounded a corner and walked into the middle of the main street of Yellow Sky. In either hand the man held a long, heavy, blue-black revolver. Often he yelled, and these cries rang through a semblance of a deserted village, shrilly flying over the roofs in a volume that seemed to have no relation to the ordinary vocal strength of a man. It was as if the surrounding stillness formed the arch of a tomb over him. These cries of ferocious challenge rang against walls of silence. And his boots had red tops with gilded imprints, of the kind beloved in winter by little sledding boys on the hillsides of New England.

The man's face flamed in a rage begot of whiskey. His eyes, rolling, and yet keen for ambush, hunted the still doorways and windows. He walked with the creeping movement of the midnight cat. As it occurred to him, he roared menacing information. The long revolvers in his hands were as easy as straws; they were moved with an electric swiftness. The little fingers of each hand played sometimes in a musician's way. Plain from the low collar of the shirt, the cords of his neck straightened and sank, straightened and sank, as passion moved him. The only sounds were his terrible invitations. The calm adobes preserved their demeanor at the passing of this small thing in the middle of the street.

There was no offer of fight—no offer of fight. The man called to the sky. There were no attractions. He bellowed and fumed and swayed his revolvers here and everywhere.

The dog of the barkeeper of the Weary Gentleman saloon had not appreciated the advance of events. He yet lay dozing in front of his master's door. At sight of the dog, the man paused and raised his revolver humorously. At sight of the man, the dog sprang up and walked diagonally away, with a sullen head, and growling. The man yelled, and the dog broke into a gallop. As it was about to enter an alley, there was a loud noise, a whistling, and something spat the ground directly before it. The dog screamed, and, wheeling in terror, galloped headlong in a new direction. Again there was a noise, a whistling, and sand was kicked viciously before it. Fear-stricken, the dog turned and flurried like an animal in a pen. The man stood laughing, his weapons at his hips.

Ultimately the man was attracted by the closed door of the Weary Gentleman saloon. He went to it and, hammering with a revolver, demanded drink.

The door remaining imperturbable, he picked a bit of paper from the walk, and nailed it to the framework with a knife. He then turned his back contemptuously upon this popular resort and, walking to the opposite side of the street and spinning there on his heel quickly and lithely, fired at the bit of paper. He missed it by a half-inch. He swore at himself, and went away. Later, he comfortably fusilladed the windows of his most intimate friend. The man was playing with this town. It was a toy for him.

But still there was no offer of fight. The name of Jack Potter, his ancient antagonist, entered his mind, and he concluded that it would be a glad thing if he should go to Potter's house, and by bombardment induce him to come out and fight. He moved in the direction of his desire, chanting Apache scalp-music.

When he arrived at it, Potter's house presented the same still front as had the other adobes. Taking up a strategic position, the man howled a challenge. But this house regarded him as might a great stone god. It gave no sign. After a decent wait, the man howled further challenges, mingling with them wonderful epithets.

Presently there came the spectacle of a man churning himself into deepest rage over the immobility of a house. He fumed at it as the winter wind attacks a prairie cabin in the North. To the distance there should have gone the sound of a tumult like the fighting of two hundred Mexicans. As necessity bade him, he paused for breath or to reload his revolvers.

IV

Potter and his bride walked sheepishly and with speed. Sometimes they laughed together shamefacedly and low.

"Next corner, dear," he said finally.

They put forth the efforts of a pair walking bowed against a strong wind. Potter was about to raise a finger to point the first appearance of the new home when, as they circled the corner, they came face to face with a man in a maroon-colored shirt, who was feverishly pushing cartridges into a large revolver. Upon the instant the man dropped his revolver to the ground, and, like lightning, whipped another from its holster. The second weapon was aimed at the bridegroom's chest.

There was a silence. Potter's mouth seemed to be merely a grave for his tongue. He exhibited an instinct to at once loosen his arm from the woman's grip, and he dropped the bag to the sand. As for the bride, her face had gone as yellow as old cloth. She was a slave to hideous rites, gazing at the apparitional snake.

The two men faced each other at a distance of three paces. He of the revolver smiled with a new and quiet ferocity.

"Tried to sneak up on me," he said. "Tried to sneak up on me!" His eyes grew more baleful. As Potter made a slight movement, the man thrust his revolver venomously forward. "No; don't you do it, Jack Potter. Don't you move a finger toward a gun just yet. Don't you move an eyelash. The time has come for me to settle with you, and I'm goin' to do it my own way, and loaf along with no interferin'. So if you don't want a gun bent on you, just mind what I tell you."

Potter looked at his enemy. "I ain't got a gun on me, Scratchy," he said. "Honest, I ain't." He was stiffening and steadying, but yet somewhere at the back of his mind a vision of the Pullman floated: the sea-green figured velvet, the shining brass, silver, and glass, the wood that gleamed as darkly brilliant as the surface of a pool of oil—all the glory of the marriage, the environment of the new estate. "You know I fight when it comes to fighting, Scratchy Wilson; but I ain't got a gun on me. You'll have to do all the shootin' yourself."

His enemy's face went livid. He stepped forward and lashed his weapon to and fro before Potter's chest. "Don't you tell me you ain't got no gun on you, you whelp. Don't tell me no lie like that. There ain't a man in Texas ever seen you without no gun. Don't take me for no kid." His eyes blazed with light, and his throat worked like a pump.

"I ain't takin' you for no kid," answered Potter. His heels had not moved an inch backward. "I'm takin' you for a d——— fool. I tell you I ain't got a gun, and I ain't. If you're goin' to shoot me up, you better begin now. You'll never get a chance like this again."

So much enforced reasoning had told on Wilson's rage. He was calmer. "If you ain't got a gun, why ain't you got a gun?" he sneered. "Been to Sunday school?"

"I ain't got a gun because I've just come from San Anton' with my wife. I'm married," said Potter. "And if I'd thought there was going to be any galoots like you prowling around when I brought my wife home, I'd had a gun, and don't you forget it."

"Married!" said Scratchy, not at all comprehending.

"Yes, married. I'm married," said Potter, distinctly.

"Married?" said Scratchy. Seemingly for the first time, he saw the drooping, drowning woman at the other man's side. "No!" he said. He was like a creature allowed a glimpse of another world. He moved a pace backward, and his arm with the revolver dropped to his side. "Is this the lady?" he asked.

"Yes, this is the lady," answered Potter.

There was another period of silence.

"Well," said Wilson at last, slowly, "I s'pose it's all off now."

"It's all off if you say so, Scratchy. You know I didn't make the trouble." Potter lifted his valise.

"Well, I 'low it's off, Jack," said Wilson. He was looking at the ground. "Married!" He was not a student of chivalry; it was merely that in the presence of this foreign condition he was a simple child of the earlier plains. He picked up his starboard revolver, and, placing both weapons in their holsters, he went away. His feet made funnel-shaped tracks in the heavy sand. ⟫

WILD WEST

Robert Boylan

Now let us speak of cowboys who on swift
White horses over blue-black deserts sped,
Their pistols blazing and their proud blood shed
In paint-flecked shanties on the haunted cliffs
Or in the bars of ghost-towns. Let us tell
The legends of fierce heroes motherless,
Not Indians, not Easterners, whose quests
And daring deeds inscribed their names in hell.
Bravely they shot it out, did Wyatt Earp,
Billy the Kid, Bill Hickok, Jesse James.
Now what remains but moving-picture dreams
Of all that fury and fast villainy?
Lone cactuses where bullets spit and ripped
The courage of the eyelid from the eye?
A rusting stirrup and a rowel thrust
Up from the calcifying sun-baked dust
Where some unknown avenger fell to sleep?
A wind-blown piece of buckskin that looked grand
When it was stretched upon the living hip
Of him who lies now six feet under ground?
Cowboys were not immortal. All they did,
Guzzling and gunning, ended when they died.

RESPONDING TO CLUSTER THREE

WHO WERE THE PEOPLE OF THE FRONTIER?

THINKING SKILL   SUMMARIZING

1. List at least five characteristics that contributed to the pioneers' survival and success. Which trait do you believe was most crucial, and why?
2. Look up "entrepreneur" in the dictionary. You can see the roots of America's entrepreneurial spirit in the first three selections in this cluster. Some say this spirit is what made the country great. Do you agree or disagree? Explain why.
3. Before the age of television, the world relied on reports from journalists and eye-witnesses for news from afar. What specific details in "Gold Rush!" and "Boomers and Sooners" succeed in making these scenes come alive?
4. "The Bride Comes to Yellow Sky" is filled with generic characters similar to the ones in Western movies. Use the chart to analyze what each character represents, and select two adjectives that **summarize** that character.

Character	Represents	Two words to summarize
Jack Potter	law and order	honorable, just
Scratchy Wilson		
The drummer		
The bride		
The bartender		
The train porter		

5. Concrete images are word-pictures that refer to the five senses: seeing, hearing, smelling, touching, and tasting. Identify two such images in the poem "Wild West." Which do you find more powerful?

Writing Activity: Character Sketch

The West was a place where people could go to reinvent themselves. If they were especially enterprising or greedy, or had unusual skills that were in demand on the frontier, they could make their fortunes or become quite powerful and important in their new communities. Write a character sketch based on one of the "types" depicted in the Cluster Three selections (gold-miner, Boomer, Sooner, frontier sheriff, gunslinger, etc.). Show how the person may have changed since coming West.

A Good Character Sketch
- places a person in a particular place and moment.
- not only describes how a person looks but how he or she moves, talks, and relates to others and the world.
- uses only those details that bring out the most important aspects of a person's character (since you can't say everything about someone in a page or two).
- uses a variety of methods of description, for example, dialogue, thoughts, and actions.

CLUSTER FOUR

Thinking on Your Own
Thinking Skill   SYNTHESIZING

MOON WALK, inspired by a NASA photograph taken during
the Apollo 17 mission to the moon, 1972

Above: Chuck Yeager, the first
man to break the sound
barrier, 1947

Right: Yeager with Sam Shepard
who played him in the 1983
film *The Right Stuff*

THE HIGH DESERT

from *The Right Stuff*

Tom Wolfe

Yeager had taken the NF–104 up for three checkout flights, edging it up gradually toward 100,000 feet, where the limits of the envelope, whatever they were, would begin to reveal themselves. And now he was out on the flight line for the second of two major preliminary flights. Tomorrow he would let it all out and go for the record. It was another of those absolutely clear brilliant afternoons on the dome of the world. In the morning flight everything had gone exactly according to plan. He had taken the ship up to 108,000 feet after cutting in the rocket engine at 60,000. The rocket had propelled the ship up at a 50-degree angle of attack. One of the disagreeable sides of the ship was her dislike of extreme angles. At any angle greater than 30 degrees, her nose would pitch up, which was the move she made just before going into spins. But at 108,000 feet it was no problem. The air was so thin at that altitude, so close to being pure "space," that the reaction controls, the hydrogen-peroxide thrusters, worked beautifully. Yeager had only to nudge the sidearm hand controller by his lap and a thruster on top of the nose of the plane pushed the nose right down again, and he was in perfect position to reenter the dense atmosphere below. Now he was going up for one final exploration of that same region before going for broke tomorrow.

At 40,000 feet Yeager began his speed run. He cut in the afterburner and it slammed him back in his seat, and he was now riding an engine with nearly 16,000 pounds of thrust. As soon as the Machmeter[1] hit

---

1 **Machmeter:** a device that measures the ratio of the speed of air to the speed of sound

2.2, he pulled back on the stick and started the climb. The afterburner would carry him to 60,000 feet before exhausting its fuel. At precisely that moment he threw the switch for the rocket engine . . . terrific jolt . . . He's slammed back in his seat again. The nose pitches up to 70 degrees. The g-forces[2] start rising. The desert sky starts falling away. He's going straight up into the indigo. At 78,000 feet a light on the console . . . as usual . . . the main engine overheating from the tremendous exertion of the climb. He throws the switch and shuts it down, but the rocket is still accelerating. Who doesn't know this feeling if he doesn't! . . . One hundred thousand feet . . . He shuts down the rocket engine. He's still climbing. The g-forces slide off . . . makes you feel like you're pitching forward . . . He's weightless, coming over the top of the arc . . . 104,000 feet . . . It's absolutely silent . . . Twenty miles up . . . The sky is almost black. He's looking straight up into it, because the nose of the ship is pitched up. His angle of attack is still about 50 degrees. He's over the top of the arc and coming down. He pushes the sidearm control to bring down the nose of the ship. Nothing happens . . . He can hear the thruster working, but the nose isn't budging. It's still pitched up. He hits the thruster again . . . She won't go down! . . . Now he can see it, the whole diagram . . . This morning at 108,000 feet the air was so thin it offered no resistance and you could easily push the nose down with the thrusters. At 104,000 feet the air remains just thick enough to exert aerodynamic pressure. The thrusters aren't strong enough to overcome it . . . He keeps hitting the reaction controls . . . The hydrogen peroxide squirts out of the jet on the nose of the ship and doesn't do a damned thing . . . He's dropping and the nose is still pitched up . . . the outside of the envelope! . . . well, here it is . . . It doesn't want to stretch . . . and here we go! . . . The ship snaps into a flat spin. It's spinning right over its center of gravity, like a pinwheel on a stick. Yeager's head is on the outer edge of the circle, spinning around. He pushes the sidearm control again. The hydrogen peroxide is finished. He has 600 pounds of fuel left in the main engine but there's no way to start it up. To relight the engine you have to put the ship nose down into a dive and force air through the intake duct and start the engine windmilling to build up rpms. Without rpms there's no

2 **g-forces:** a measure of force on a body undergoing acceleration; g stands for the acceleration of gravity

hydraulic pressure and without hydraulic pressure you can't move the stabilizer wings on the tail and without the stabilizer wings you can't control the plane at the lower altitudes . . . He's in a steady-state flat spin and dropping . . . He's whirling around at a terrific rate . . . He makes himself keep his eyes pinned on the instruments . . . A little sightseeing at this point and it's vertigo and you're finished . . . He's down to 80,000 feet and the rpms are at dead zero . . . He's falling 150 feet a second . . . 9,000 feet a minute . . . *And what do I do next?* . . . here in the jaws of the Gulp . . . *I've tried A!—I've tried B!*—The beast isn't making a sound . . . just spinning around like a length of pipe in the sky . . . He has one last shot . . . the speed brakes, a parachute rig in the tail for slowing the ship down after a high-speed landing . . . The altimeter keeps winding down . . . Twenty-five thousand feet . . . but the altimeter is based on sea level . . . . He's only 21,000 feet above the high desert . . . The slack's running out . . He pops the speed brake . . . *Bango!*—the chute catches with a jolt . . . It pulls the tail up . . . He pitches down . . . The spin stops. The nose is pointed down. Now he only has to jettison the chute and let her dive and kick up the rpms. He jettisons the chute . . . and the beast heaves up again! The nose goes back up in the air! . . . It's the rear stabilizer wing . . . The leading edge is locked, frozen into the position of the climb to altitude. With no rpms and no hydraulic controls he can't move the tail . . . The nose is pitched way above 30 degrees . . . Here she goes again . . . She's back into the spin . . . He's spinning out on the rim again . . . He has no rpms, no power, no more speed chute, and only 180 knots airspeed . . . He's down to 12,000 feet . . . 8,000 feet above the farm[3] . . . There's not a damned thing left in the manual or the bag of tricks or the righteous-ness of twenty years of military flying . . . Chosen or damned! . . . It blows at any seam! Yeager hasn't bailed out of an airplane since the day he was shot down over Germany when he was twenty . . . I've tried A!—I've tried B!—I've tried C! . . . 11,000 feet, 7,000 from the farm . . . He hunches himself into a ball, just as it says in the manual, and reaches under the seat for the cinch ring and pulls . . . He's exploded out of the cockpit with such force it's like a concussion . . . He can't see . . . *Wham.* . . a jolt in back . . . It's the seat separating from him and

---

3 **the farm:** a shortened version of the slang phrase "bought the farm," meaning died

the parachute rig . . . His head begins to clear . . . He's in midair, in his pressure suit, looking out through the visor of his helmet . . . Every second seems enormously elongated . . . infinite . . . such slow motion . . . He's suspended in midair . . . weightless . . . The ship had been falling at about 100 miles an hour and the ejection rocket had propelled him up at 90 miles an hour. For one thick adrenal moment he's weightless in midair, 7,000 feet above the desert . . . The seat floats nearby, as if the two of them are parked in the atmosphere . . . The butt of the seat, the underside, is facing him . . . a red hole . . . the socket where the ejection mechanism had been attached . . . It's dribbling a charcoal red. . . lava . . . the remains of the rocket propellant . . . It's glowing . . . it's oozing out of the socket . . . In the next moment they're both falling, him and the seat . . . His parachute rig has a quarter bag over it and on the bag is a drogue chute that pulls the bag off so the parachute will stream out gradually and not break the chute or the pilot's back when the canopy pops open during a high-speed ejection. It's designed for an ejection at 400 or 500 miles an hour but he's only going about 175. In this infinitely expanded few seconds the lines stream out and Yeager and the rocket seat and the glowing red socket sail through the air together . . . and now the seat is drifting above him . . . into the chute lines! . . . The seat is nestled in the chute lines . . . dribbling lava out of the socket . . . eating through the lines . . . An infinite second . . . He's jerked up by the shoulders . . . it's the chute opening and the canopy filling . . . in that very instant *the lava*—it smashes into the visor of his helmet . . . Something slices through his left eye . . . He's knocked silly . . . He can't see a damned thing . . . The burning snaps him to . . . His left eye is gushing blood . . . It's pouring down inside the lid and down his face and his face is on fire . . . the seat rig . . . The jerk of the parachute had suddenly slowed his speed, but the seat kept falling . . . It had fallen out of the chute lines and the butt end crashed into his visor . . . 180 pounds of metal . . . a double visor . . . the damned thing has smashed through both layers . . . He's burning! . . . There's rocket lava inside the helmet . . . The seat has fallen away . . . He can't see . . . blood pouring out of his left eye and there's smoke inside the helmet . . . Rubber! . . . It's the seal between the helmet and the pressure suit . . . It's burning up . . . The propellant won't quit . . . A tremendous *whoosh* . . . He can feel the rush . . . He can even hear it . . . The whole left side of the helmet is full of flames . . . A sheet of flame goes up his neck and the side of his face . . . The oxygen! . . . The propellant has burned through the rubber seal, setting off the pressure suit's automatic oxygen system . . . The integrity of the circuit has been violated and it rushes oxygen to the helmet, to the pilot's face . . . A hundred percent oxygen! . . . It turns the lava into a burning inferno . . . Everything that can burn is on fire . . . everything else is melting . . . Even with the hole smashed in the visor the helmet is full of smoke . . . He's choking . . . blinded . . . The left side of his head is on fire . . . He's suffocating . . . He brings up his left hand . . . He has on pressure-suit gloves locked and taped to the sleeve . . . He jams his hand in through the hold in the visor and tries to create an air scoop with it to bring air to his mouth . . . The flames . . . They're all over it . . . They go to work on the glove where it touches his face . . . They devour it . . .His index finger is burning up . . . His damned finger is burning! . . . But he doesn't move it . . . Get some air! . . . Nothing else matters . . . He's gulping smoke . . . He has to get the visor open . . . It's twisted . . . He's encased in a little broken globe dying in a cloud of his own fried flesh . . . The stench of it! . . . rubber and a human hide. . . He has to get the visor open . . . It's that or nothing, no two ways about it . . . It's smashed all to hell . . . He jams both hands underneath . . . It's a tremendous effort. . . It lifts . . . Salvation! . . . Like a sea the air carries it all away, the smoke, the flames . . . The fire is out. He can breathe. He can see out of his right eye. The desert, the mesquite, the motherless Joshua trees are rising slowly toward him . . . He can't open his left eye . . . Now he can feel the pain . . . Half his head is broiled . . . That isn't the worst of it . . . The damned finger! . . . He can make out the terrain, he's been over it a million times . . . Over there's the highway, 466, and there's Route 6 crossing it . . . His left glove is practically burned off . . . The glove and his left index finger . . . he can't tell them apart . . . they look as if they exploded in an oven . . . He's not far from base . . . Whatever it is with the finger, it's very bad . . . Nearly down . . . He gets ready . . . Right out of the manual . . . A terrific wallop . . . He's down on the mesquite, looking across the desert, one-eyed . . . He stands up . . . He's in one piece! . . . He can hardly use his left hand. The finger is killing him. The whole side of his head . . . He starts taking off the parachute harness . . . It's all in the manual! Regulation issue! . . . He starts rolling up the parachute, just like it says . . . Some of the cords are almost melted through, from the lava . . . His head feels like it's still on fire . . . The pain comes from way down deep . . But he's got to get the helmet off . . . It's a hell of an operation . . . He doesn't dare touch his head . . . It feels enormous . . . Somebody's running toward him . . . It's a kid, a guy in his twenties . . . He's come from the highway . . . He comes up close and his mouth falls open and he gives Yeager a look of stone horror . . .

"Are you all right!"

The look on the kid's face!. . .

"I was in my car! I saw you coming down!"

"Listen," says Yeager. The pain in his finger is terrific. "Listen. . . you got a knife?"

The kid digs into his pocket and pulls out a penknife. Yeager starts cutting the glove off his left hand. He can't bear it any more. The kid stands there hypnotized and horrified. From the look on the kid's face, Yeager can begin to see himself. His neck, the whole left side of his head, his ear, his cheek, his eye must be burned up. His eye socket is slashed, swollen, caked shut, and covered with a crust of burned blood, and half his hair is burned away. The whole mess and the rest of his face and his nostril and his lips are smeared with the sludge of the burning rubber. And he's standing there in the middle of the desert in a pressure suit with his head cocked, squinting out of one eye, working on his left glove with a penknife . . . The knife cuts through the glove and it cuts through the meat of his finger . . . You can't tell any longer. . . It's all run together . . . The finger looks like it's melted. . . He's got to get the glove off. That's all there is to it. It hurts too much. He pulls off the glove and a big hunk of melted meat from the finger comes off with it . . . It's like fried suet . . .

"Arrggghhh . . . " It's the kid. He's retching. It's too much for him. He looks up at Yeager. His eyes open and his mouth opens. All the glue has come undone. He can't hold it together any longer.

"God," he says, "you . . . look *awful!*" The Good Samaritan, A.A.D.! Also a Doctor! And he just gave his diagnosis! That's all a man needs . . . to be forty years old and to fall one hundred thousand feet in a flat spin and punch out and make a million-dollar hole in the ground and get half his head and his hand burned up and have his eye practically ripped out of his skull . . . and have the Good Samaritan, A.A.D., arrive as if sent by the spirit of Pancho Barnes herself to render a midnight verdict among the motherless Joshua trees while the screen doors bang and the pictures of a hundred dead pilots rattle in their frames:[4]

"My God! . . . you look awful."

A few minutes later the rescue helicopter arrived. The medics found Yeager standing out in the mesquite, him and some kid who had been passing by. Yeager was standing erect with his parachute rolled up and his helmet in the crook of his arm, right out of the manual, and staring at them quite levelly out of what was the left of his face, as if they had had an appointment and he was on time.

At the hospital they discovered one stroke of good luck. The blood over Yeager's left eye had been baked into a crustlike shield. Otherwise he might have lost it. He had suffered third- and second-degree burns on his head and neck. The burns required a month of treatment in the hospital, but he was able to heal without disfigurement. He even regained full use of his left index finger.

It so happened that on the day of Yeager's flight, at just about the time he headed down the runway on takeoff, the Secretary of Defense, Robert McNamara, announced that the X–20 program had been canceled. Although the Manned Orbiting Laboratory scheme remained alive officially, it was pretty obvious that there would be no American military space voyagers. The boys in Houston had the only ticket: the top of the pyramid was theirs to extend to the stars, if they were able.

Yeager was returned to flight status and resumed his duties at ARPS. In time, he would go on to fly more than a hundred missions in Southeast Asia in B–57 tactical bombers.

No one ever broke the Russian mark with the NF–104 or even tried to. Up above 100,000 feet the plane's envelope was full of holes. And Yeager never again sought to set a record in the sky over the high desert. ☙

---

4 **Pancho Barnes . . . a hundred dead pilots rattle in their frames:**
Barnes ran a bar called the Fly Inn near the base from which Yeager took off. On its walls were photographs of test pilots who died.

124

AT THE ELECTRONIC FRONTIER

Miguel Algarín

I search the chemistry of specific emotions,
a combination of earth and air
that evokes the vital detail,
the phrase that heats the frying pan,
the look that smiles,
offering signals that localize,
where I am, and clarify what I see.
I'm a child of the Electronic Frontier.
I learn off the radio waves
of 98.7 Kiss F.M. salsa/disco jams,
that come from a Sony,
bought even though I need a coat,
even though I'm behind on my payments
for the Trinitron Remote Control Color T.V.
that I picked up at Crazy Eddie's last month.
I'm a child of the Columbia Space Shuttle,
and I need to know all the electronic gimmicks
invented yesterday
that are already primitive cousins
to those developed today
from eight to five P.M. in Japan.

VOYAGE TO THE LAST FRONTIER

Michael D. Lemonick

It flies like an underwater bird, capable of skimming just beneath the ocean's surface or plunging thousands of feet below it. Named Deep Flight I, this revolutionary new undersea vessel is shaped like a chubby, winged torpedo, 12 feet long and weighing 3500 pounds. With a touch of the controls, a skilled pilot—who lies prone in a body harness, his or her head protruding into the craft's glass nose—can perform barrel rolls, race a fast-moving pod of whales or leap vertically right out of the water.

But Deep Flight I is just a pale prototype of the ocean-exploring vessels to come. Back in their Point Richmond, Calif., workshop, the craft's designers have already drawn blueprints for its successor, Deep Flight II, an ocean submersible capable of diving not just a few thousand feet but as far as seven miles straight down, the aquatic equivalent of reaching Mount Everest or the South Pole or the moon.

More than 35 years after the bathyscaph Trieste, a watertight sphere, took two men 35,800 feet down to the deepest spot in the world—the Mariana Trench just south of Guam in the western Pacific—undersea adventurers are preparing to go back. Last March a Japanese robot scouted a tiny portion of the bottom of the crevasse, which is more than 1580 miles long, and sent back the first real time video images of deepest-sea life.

We've reached Mount Everest, the 29,028-foot pinnacle of the Himalayas, more than 100 times. Manned voyages to space have become commonplace, and robot probes have ventured to the outer reaches of the solar system. Now, in laboratories around the world, engineers are hard at work on sophisticated craft designed to explore the last great unconquered frontier on earth: the bottom of the sea.

"There's a perception that we have already explored the sea," says marine biologist Sylvia Earle, a former chief scientist at the National Oceanographic and Atmospheric Administration in Washington, D.C. "The reality is that we know more about Mars than we know about the oceans."

There's a lot to explore. Oceans cover nearly three-quarters of the planet's surface—over 320 million cubic miles of water that reach an average depth of 2.3 miles. The sea's intricate food webs support more life by weight and a greater diversity of animals than any other ecosystem. Somewhere below, there even lurks the last certified sea monster left from prescientific times: the 64-foot-long giant squid.

The push to reach the bottom of the sea has fired the imagination of some of the world's most daring explorers. It's a high-sea adventure fraught with danger and controversy. But the potential rewards make it all worthwhile: oil and mineral wealth to rival Alaska's North Slope and California's Gold Rush; scientific discoveries that could change our view of how the planet—and life on it—evolved; natural substances that could yield new medicines and whole new classes of industrial chemicals.

Majestically swirling ocean currents influence much of the world's weather patterns. Figuring out how they operate could save trillions of dollars in weather-related disasters. The oceans also have vast reserves of nickel, iron, manganese, copper and cobalt. Pharmaceutical and biotechnology companies are already analyzing deep-sea bacteria, fish and marine plants, looking for future miracle drugs.

Says Bruce Robison of the Monterey Bay Aquarium Research Institute in California: "The discoveries beneficial to mankind will far outweigh those of the space program. If we can get to the abyss regularly, there will be immediate payoffs."

In the wake of the U.S. Navy bathyscaph Treiste's 1960 dive, the number of submersibles expanded dramatically, with the Soviet Union,

France and Japan each building its own. For the first time, scientists could systematically collect animals, plants and rocks rather than study whatever they dredged up in baskets that had been lowered from the surface. Thus began a remarkable period of undersea discovery that has transformed biology, geology and oceanography.

Scientists have learned that the seas hold canyons deep enough to hide the Himalayas. They are also the setting for the largest geologic feature on the planet: a globe-circling, 34,000-mile-long mountain range that makes its way through the Atlantic, Pacific, Indian and Arctic oceans.

This range supports the theory of plate tec-  tonics, according to which the surface of the earth is a series of hard "plates" floating on a bed of partly molten rock. The mid-ocean ridges, geologists argued, were likely locations for planetary crust to be created: the new plate material would be pushed upward by forces from below before it settled back down to form the sea floor. An even more dramatic confirmation came from the Pacific, where black clouds of superheated, mineral-rich water were discovered spewing from chim- neylike mounds on the bottom of the ocean. Occurring at typical depths of 7300 feet, these hot gushers, known as hydrothermal vents, work much the same way Yellowstone National Park's Old Faithful does. Sea water percolates down through cracks in the crust, getting progressively hotter. Finally, the hot water gushes back up in murky clouds that cool rapidly, dumping dis- solved minerals—including zinc, copper, iron, sulfur compounds and silica—onto the ocean floor.

Scientists were also astonished to learn that some of these hydrothermal vents are bursting with life. On a dive off the Galápagos in 1977, researchers found the water around a vent teeming with bac- teria and surrounded by peculiar 30-inch-long worms, clams the size of dinner plates, mussels and a strange pink-skinned, blue-eyed fish.

What were these animals feeding on in the absence of any detectable food supply? How were they surviving without light?

The answer, surprisingly, was that the bacteria were chemosynthetic—as opposed to photosynthetic—getting their energy from chemicals rather than the sun. They were living inside the mollusks and worms, breaking down chemicals into usable food—an ecological niche nobody had suspected they could fill. Many biologists now believe that the very first organisms on earth were similarly chemosynthetic. Therefore, the vents may well be the best laboratory available for studying how life on the planet actually began.

Both scientists and policymakers debate the value of deep-sea exploration. Only the richest countries can afford to explore. Leading the quest for the bottom is Japan, which has a compelling need to understand the ocean floor: the southern part of the island nation sits on the meeting place of three tectonic plates. As these plates grind against one another, they generate about one percent of the world's earthquakes of magnitude five or higher, including the 1995 quake that killed 5502 people in Kobe.

Because of its desperate need to anticipate future quakes, Japan built the Shinkai 6500 submersible, which can go deeper than any piloted craft in the world. On its first series of missions in 1991, the Shinkai 6500 found deep fissures on the edge of the Pacific plate, which presses on the islands from the east. And, with an unmanned 11-ton, $53.4-million remotely operated vehicle called Kaiko, the Japanese have gone all the way to the deepest reaches of the ocean. Kaiko puts scientists on the scene through video images, enabling them to gather around a monitor and discuss what they are seeing.

The cheapest way to explore the ocean floor, however, may be with the free-swimming autonomous underwater vehicles. AUVS can roam the depths without human intervention for as long as a year, patiently accumulating data. Two American AUVS—a government and university-funded craft called Odyssey and the Autonomous Benthic Explorer from Woods Hole, Mass.—completed tests in the past two years off the coast of Washington and Oregon. Eventually, fleets of these underwater robots will be able to communicate among themselves, periodically beaming their data to researchers on shore.

Funding is always a problem, however. In the United States, the government is giving less money to civilian scientists. The most innovative designs in underwater craft are coming from private companies building for the oil and gas industry, various navies, universities and even film crews. The Deep Flight I vehicle, built by British engineer Graham Hawkes, was financed by several film and television firms and a marine-archaeology company. When Deep Flight II is finished, Hawkes hopes trips to the deepest abyss could become almost routine.

* * *

Despite the budget cuts, the inhospitable environment and the pressing danger, there is little doubt that humans, one way or another, are headed to the bottom of the sea. The rewards of exploring the coldest, darkest waters—scientific, economic and psychological—are just too great to pass up. Ultimately, people will go to the abyss for the same reason that climbers have scaled Everest: because it's there. ❧

THE MILLION-YEAR PICNIC

Ray Bradbury

Somehow the idea was brought up by Mom that perhaps the whole family would enjoy a fishing trip. But they weren't Mom's words; Timothy knew that. They were Dad's words, and Mom used them for him somehow.

Dad shuffled his feet in a clutter of Martian pebbles and agreed. So immediately there was a tumult and a shouting, and very quickly the camp was tucked into capsules and containers, Mom slipped into traveling jumpers and blouse, Dad stuffed his pipe full with trembling hands, his eyes on the Martian sky, and the three boys piled yelling into the motorboat, none of them really keeping an eye on Mom and Dad, except Timothy.

Dad pushed a stud. The water boat sent a humming sound up into the sky. The water shook back and the boat nosed ahead, and the family cried, "Hurrah!"

Timothy sat in the back of the boat with Dad, his small fingers atop Dad's hairy ones, watching the canal twist, leaving the crumbled place behind where they had landed in their small family rocket all the way from Earth. He remembered the night before they left Earth, the hustling and hurrying, the rocket that Dad had found somewhere, somehow, and the talk of a vacation on Mars. A long way to go for a vacation, but Timothy said nothing because of his younger brothers. They came to Mars and now, first thing, or so they said, they were going fishing.

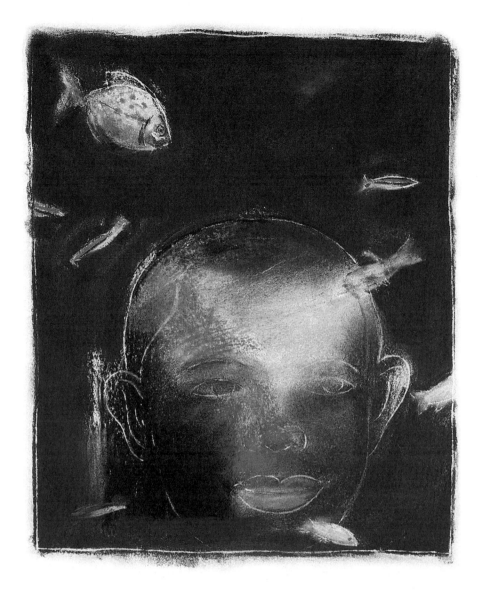

Dad had a funny look in his eyes as the boat went up-canal. A look that Timothy couldn't figure. It was made of strong light and maybe a sort of relief. It made the deep wrinkles laugh instead of worry or cry.

So there went the cooling rocket, around a bend, gone.

"How far are we going?" Robert splashed his hand. It looked like a small crab jumping in the violet water.

Dad exhaled. "A million years."

"Gee," said Robert.

"Look, kids." Mother pointed one soft long arm. "There's a dead city."

They looked with fervent anticipation, and the dead city lay dead for them alone, drowsing in a hot silence of summer made on Mars by a Martian weatherman.

And Dad looked as if he was pleased that it was dead.

It was a futile spread of pink rocks sleeping on a rise of sand, a few tumbled pillars, one lonely shrine, and then the sweep of sand again. Nothing else for miles. A white desert around the canal and a blue desert over it.

Just then a bird flew up. Like a stone thrown across a blue pond, hitting, falling deep, and vanishing.

Dad got a frightened look when he saw it. "I thought it was a rocket."

Timothy looked at the deep ocean sky, trying to see Earth and the war and the ruined cities and the men killing each other since the day he was born. But he saw nothing. The war was as removed and far off as two flies battling to the death in the arch of a great high and silent cathedral. And just as senseless.

William Thomas wiped his forehead and felt the touch of his son's hand on his arm, like a young tarantula, thrilled. He beamed at his son. "How goes it, Timmy?"

"Fine, Dad."

Timothy hadn't quite figured out what was ticking inside the vast adult mechanism beside him. The man with the immense hawk nose, sunburnt, peeling—and the hot blue eyes like agate marbles you play with after school in summer back on Earth, and the long thick columnar legs in the loose riding breeches.

"What are you looking at so hard, Dad?"

"I was looking for Earthian logic, common sense, good government, peace, and responsibility."

"All that up there?"

"No. I didn't find it. It's not there any more. Maybe it'll never be there again. Maybe we fooled ourselves that it was ever there."

"Huh?"

"See the fish," said Dad, pointing.

* * *

There rose a soprano clamor from all three boys as they rocked the boat in arching their tender necks to see. They *oohed* and *ahed*. A silver ring fish floated by them, undulating, and closing like an iris, instantly, around food particles, to assimilate them.

Dad looked at it. His voice was deep and quiet.

"Just like war. War swims along, sees food, contracts. A moment later—Earth is gone."

"William," said Mom.

"Sorry," said Dad.

They sat still and felt the canal water rush cool, swift, and glassy. The only sound was the motor hum, the glide of water, the sun expanding the air.

"When do we see the Martians?" cried Michael.

"Quite soon, perhaps," said Father. "Maybe tonight."

"Oh, but the Martians are a dead race now," said Mom.

"No, they're not. I'll show you some Martians, all right," Dad said presently.

Timothy scowled at that but said nothing. Everything was odd now. Vacations and fishing and looks between people.

The other boys were already engaged making shelves of their small hands and peering under them toward the seven-foot stone banks of the canal, watching for Martians.

"What do they look like?" demanded Michael.

"You'll know them when you see them." Dad sort of laughed, and Timothy saw a pulse beating time in his cheek.

Mother was slender and soft, with a woven plait of spun-gold hair over her head in a tiara, and eyes the color of the deep cool canal water where it ran in shadow, almost purple, with flecks of amber caught in it. You could see her thoughts swimming around in her eyes, like fish— some bright, some dark, some fast, quick, some slow and easy, and sometimes, like when she looked up where Earth was, being nothing but color and nothing else. She sat in the boat's prow, one hand resting on the side lip, the other on the lap of her dark blue breeches, and a line of sunburnt soft neck showing where her blouse opened like a white flower.

She kept looking ahead to see what was there, and, not being able to see it clearly enough, she looked backward toward her husband, and through his eyes, reflected then, she saw what was ahead; and since he added part of himself to this reflection, a determined firmness, her face relaxed and she accepted it and she turned back, knowing suddenly what to look for.

Timothy looked too. But all he saw was a straight pencil line of canal going violet through a wide shallow valley penned by low, eroded hills, and on until it fell over the sky's edge. And this canal went on and on, through cities that would have rattled like beetles in a dry skull if you shook them. A hundred or two hundred cities dreaming hot summer-day dreams and cool summer-night dreams . . .

They had come millions of miles for this outing—to fish. But there had been a gun on the rocket. This was a vacation. But why all the food, more than enough to last them years and years, left hidden back there near the rocket? Vacation. Just behind the veil of the vacation was not a soft face of laughter, but something hard and bony and perhaps terrifying. Timothy could not lift the veil, and the two other boys were busy being ten and eight years old, respectively.

"No Martians yet. Nuts." Robert put his V-shaped chin on his hands and glared at the canal.

Dad had brought an atomic radio along, strapped to his wrist. It functioned on an old-fashioned principle: you held it against the bones near your ear and it vibrated singing or talking to you. Dad listened to it now. His face looked like one of those fallen Martian cities, caved in, sucked dry, almost dead.

Then he gave it to Mom to listen. Her lips dropped open.

"What—" Timothy started to question, but never finished what he wished to say.

For at that moment there were two titanic, marrow-jolting explosions that grew upon themselves, followed by a half-dozen minor concussions.

Jerking his head up, Dad notched the boat speed higher immediately. The boat leaped and jounced and spanked. This shook Robert out of his funk and elicited yelps of frightened but ecstatic joy from Michael, who clung to Mom's legs and watched the water pour by his nose in a wet torrent.

Dad swerved the boat, cut speed, and ducked the craft into a little branch canal and under an ancient, crumbling stone wharf that smelled of crab flesh. The boat rammed the wharf hard enough to throw them all forward, but no one was hurt, and Dad was already twisted to see if the ripples on the canal were enough to map their route into hiding. Water lines went across, lapped the stones, and rippled back to meet each other, settling, to be dappled by the sun. It all went away.

Dad listened. So did everybody.

Dad's breathing echoed like fists beating against the cold wet wharf stones. In the shadow, Mom's cat eyes just watched Father for some clue to what next.

Dad relaxed and blew out a breath, laughing at himself.

"The rocket, of course. I'm getting jumpy. The rocket."

Michael said, "What happened, Dad, what happened?"

"Oh, we just blew up our rocket, is all," said Timothy, trying to sound matter-of-fact. "I've heard rockets blown up before. Ours just blew."

"Why did we blow up our rocket?" asked Michael. "Huh, Dad?"

"It's part of the game, silly!" said Timothy.

"A game!" Michael and Robert loved the word.

"Dad fixed it so it would blow up and no one'd know where we landed or went! In case they ever came looking, see?"

"Oh boy, a secret!"

"Scared by my own rocket," admitted Dad to Mom. "I am nervous. It's silly to think there'll ever *be* any more rockets. Except *one*, perhaps, if Edwards and his wife get through with *their* ship."

He put his tiny radio to his ear again. After two minutes he dropped his hand as you would drop a rag.

"It's over at last," he said to Mom. "The radio just went off the atomic beam. Every other world station's gone. They dwindled down to a couple in the last few years. Now the air's completely silent. It'll probably remain silent."

"For how long?" asked Robert.

"Maybe—your great-grandchildren will hear it again," said Dad. He just sat there, and the children were caught in the center of his awe and defeat and resignation and acceptance.

Finally he put the boat out into the canal again, and they continued in the direction in which they had originally started.

It was getting late. Already the sun was down the sky, and a series of dead cities lay ahead of them.

Dad talked very quietly and gently to his sons. Many times in the past he had been brisk, distant, removed from them, but now he patted them on the head with just a word and they felt it.

"Mike, pick a city."

"What, Dad?"

"Pick a city, Son. Any one of these cities we pass."

"All right," said Michael. "How do I pick?'

"Pick the one you like the most. You, too, Robert and Tim. Pick the city you like best."

"I want a city with Martians in it," said Michael.

"You'll have that," said Dad. "I promise." His lips were for the children, but his eyes were for Mom.

They passed six cities in twenty minutes. Dad didn't say anything more about the explosions; he seemed much more interested in having fun with his sons, keeping them happy, than anything else.

Michael liked the first city they passed, but this was vetoed because everyone doubted quick first judgments. The second city nobody liked. It was an Earth Man's settlement, built of wood and already rotting into sawdust. Timothy liked the third city because it was large. The fourth and fifth were too small and the sixth brought acclaim from everyone, including Mother, who joined in the Gees, Goshes, and Look-at-thats!

There were fifty or sixty huge structures still standing, streets were dusty but paved, and you could see one or two old centrifugal fountains still pulsing wetly in the plazas. That was the only life—water leaping in the late sunlight.

"This is the city," said everybody.

Steering the boat to a wharf, Dad jumped out.

"Here we are. This is ours. This is where we live from now on!"

"From now on?" Michael was incredulous. He stood up, looking, and then turned to blink back at where the rocket used to be. "What about the rocket? What about Minnesota?"

"Here," said Dad.

He touched the small radio to Michael's blond head. "Listen."

Michael listened.

"Nothing," he said.

"That's right. Nothing. Nothing at all any more. No more Minneapolis, no more rockets, no more Earth."

Michael considered the lethal revelation and began to sob little dry sobs.

"Wait a moment," said Dad the next instant. "I'm giving you a lot more in exchange, Mike!"

"What?" Michael held off the tears, curious, but quite ready to continue in case Dad's further revelation was as disconcerting as the original.

"I'm giving you this city, Mike. It's yours."

"Mine?"

"For you and Robert and Timothy, all three of you, to own for yourselves."

Timothy bounded from the boat. "Look, guys, all for *us*! All of *that*!" He was playing the game with Dad, playing it large and playing it well. Later, after it was all over and things had settled, he could go off by himself and cry for ten minutes. But now it was still a game, still a family outing, and the other kids must be kept playing.

Mike jumped out with Robert. They helped Mom.

"Be careful of your sister," said Dad, and nobody knew what he meant until later.

They hurried into the great pink-stoned city, whispering among themselves, because dead cities have a way of making you want to whisper, to watch the sun go down.

"In about five days," said Dad quietly, "I'll go back down to where our rocket was and collect the food hidden in the ruins there and bring it here; and I'll hunt for Bert Edwards and his wife and daughters there."

"Daughters?" asked Timothy. "How many?"

"Four."

"I can see that'll cause trouble later." Mom nodded slowly.

"Girls." Michael made a face like an ancient Martian stone image. "Girls."

"Are they coming in a rocket, too?"

"Yes. If they make it. Family rockets are made for travel to the Moon, not Mars. We were lucky we got through."

"Where did you get the rocket?" whispered Timothy, for the other boys were running ahead.

"I saved it. I saved it for twenty years, Tim. I had it hidden away, hoping I'd never have to use it. I suppose I should have given it to the government for the war, but I kept thinking about Mars. . . ."

"And a picnic!"

"Right. This is between you and me. When I saw everything was finishing on Earth, after I'd waited until the last moment, I packed us up. Bert Edwards had a ship hidden, too, but we decided it would be safer to take off separately, in case anyone tried to shoot us down."

"Why'd you blow up the rocket, Dad?"

"So we can't go back, ever. And so if any of those evil men ever come to Mars they won't know we're here."

"Is that why you look up all the time?'

"Yes, it's silly. They won't follow us, ever. They haven't anything to follow with. I'm being too careful, is all."

Michael came running back. "Is this really *our* city, Dad?"

"The whole darn planet belongs to us, kids. The whole darn planet."

They stood there, King of the Hill, Top of the Heap, Ruler of All They Surveyed, Unimpeachable Monarchs and Presidents, trying to understand what it meant to own a world and how big a world really was.

Night came quickly in the thin atmosphere, and Dad left them in the square by the pulsing fountain, went down to the boat, and came walking back carrying a stack of paper in his big hands.

He laid the papers in a clutter in an old courtyard and set them afire. To keep warm, they crouched around the blaze and laughed, and Timothy saw the little letters leap like frightened animals when the flames touched and engulfed them. The papers crinkled like an old man's skin, and the cremation surrounded innumerable words:

"GOVERNMENT BONDS; Business Graph, 1999; Religious Prejudice: An Essay; The Science of Logistics; Problems of the Pan-American Unity; Stock Report for July 3, 1998; The War Digest . . ."

Dad had insisted on bringing these papers for this purpose. He sat there and fed them into the fire, one by one, with satisfaction, and told his children what it all meant.

"It's time I told you a few things. I don't suppose it was fair, keeping so much from you. I don't know if you'll understand, but I have to talk, even if only part of it gets over to you."

He dropped a leaf in the fire.

"I'm burning a way of life, just like that way of life is being burned clean of Earth right now. Forgive me if I talk like a politician. I am, after all, a former state governor, and I was honest and they hated me for it. Life on Earth never settled down to doing anything very good. Science ran too far ahead of us too quickly, and the people got lost in a mechanical wilderness, like children making over pretty things, gadgets, helicopters, rockets; emphasizing the wrong items, emphasizing machines instead of how to run the machines. Wars got bigger and bigger and finally killed Earth. That's what the silent radio means. That's what we ran away from.

"We were lucky. There aren't any more rockets left. It's time you knew this isn't a fishing trip at all. I put off telling you. Earth is gone. Interplanetary travel won't be back for centuries, maybe never. But that way of life proved itself wrong and strangled itself with its own hands. You're young. I'll tell you this again every day until it sinks in."

He paused to feed more papers to the fire.

"Now we're alone. We and a handful of others who'll land in a few days. Enough to start over. Enough to turn away from all that back on Earth and strike out on a new line—"

The fire leaped up to emphasize his talking. And then all the papers were gone except one. All the laws and beliefs of Earth were burnt into small hot ashes which soon would be carried off in a wind.

Timothy looked at the last thing that Dad tossed in the fire. It was a map of the World, and it wrinkled and distorted itself hotly and went— flimpf—and was gone like a warm, black butterfly. Timothy turned away.

"Now I'm going to show you the Martians," said Dad. "Come on, all of you. Here, Alice." He took her hand.

Michael was crying loudly, and Dad picked him up and carried him, and they walked down through the ruins toward the canal.

The canal. Where tomorrow or the next day their future wives would come up in a boat, small laughing girls now, with their father and mother.

The night came down around them, and there were stars. But Timothy couldn't find Earth. It had already set. That was something to think about.

A night bird called among the ruins as they walked. Dad said, "Your mother and I will try to teach you. Perhaps we'll fail. I hope not. We've had a good lot to see and learn from. We planned this trip years ago, before you were born. Even if there hadn't been a war we would have come to Mars, I think, to live and form our own standard of living. It would have been another century before Mars would have been really poisoned by the Earth civilization. Now, of course—"

They reached the canal. It was long and straight and cool and wet and reflective in the night.

"I've always wanted to see a Martian," said Michael. "Where are they, Dad? You promised."

"There they are," said Dad, and he shifted Michael on his shoulder and pointed straight down.

The Martians were there. Timothy began to shiver.

The Martians were there—in the canal—reflected in the water. Timothy and Michael and Robert and Mom and Dad.

The Martians stared back up at them for a long, long silent time from the rippling water. . . . ❧

Responding to Cluster Four
Thinking Skill SYNTHESIZING

1. Each of the other clusters in this book is introduced by a question that is meant to help readers focus their thinking about the selections. What do you think the question for Cluster Four should be?

2. How do you think the selections in this cluster should be taught? Demonstrate your ideas by joining with your classmates to: a) create discussion questions b) lead discussions about the selections c) develop vocabulary quizzes d) prepare a cluster quiz.

Responding to WIDE OPEN SPACES:
Essential Question WHAT IS THE LURE OF THE FRONTIER?

Reflecting on this book as a whole provides an opportunity for independent learning and the application of the critical thinking skill, synthesis. *Synthesizing* means examining all the things you have learned from this book and combining them to form a richer and more meaningful view of the Westward expansion movement and American frontiers.

There are many ways to demonstrate what you know about America's frontiers. Here are some possibilities. Your teacher may provide others.

1. What advances have there been on the technological frontier since you were born? Write an essay or speech describing how discoveries on the modern frontiers of cyberspace or elsewhere have changed ordinary citizens' daily lives and expectations.

2. Manifest Destiny and the ideals it embodied changed the way Americans thought about the North American continent. With the purchase of Louisiana Territory, Americans began thinking of themselves not simply as citizens of the 13 former colonies on the Atlantic Coast, but as citizens of a new nation with limitless land and opportunity for those who had the vision to move West. Stage a debate on one of the following issues:

   Resolved: Manifest Destiny and the ideas it embodied helped to make America stronger.

   Resolved: American Indians should be reimbursed for the lands taken from them by the American government.

ACKNOWLEDGEMENTS

TEXT CREDITS CONTINUED FROM PAGE 2 "The Million Year Picnic" reprinted by permission of Don Congdon Associates, Inc. Copyright © 1946, renewed 1974 by Ray Bradbury.

"Tsali of the Cherokees" from American Indian Mythology by Alice Marriott. Copyright © 1968 by Alice Marriott and Carol K. Rachlin. Reprinted by permission of HarperCollins Publishers, Inc.

"Voyage to the Last Frontier" by Michael D. Lemonick, Copyright © 1995 Time Inc. Reprinted by permission.

"Where West Is" by Thom Tammaro first appeared in Quarterly West, copyright © 1976 by Thom Tammaro. Reprinted with permission of the author.

Excerpt from "The High Desert" from The Right Stuff by Tom Wolfe, Copyright © 1979 by Tom Wolfe. Reprinted by permission of Farrar, Straus and Giroux, LLC.

"Daniel Boone" by Arthur Guiterman from I Sing the Pioneer, Copyright © 1926. Reprinted by permission of Louise H. Sclove.

"Journals of the Lewis and Clark Expedition" includes

For September 17, 1804, September 25, 1804, April 14, 1805
Reprinted from The Journals of Lewis and Clark Expedition, volume 3, edited by Gary Moulton by permission of the University of Nebraska Press. Copyright © 1987 by the University of Nebraska Press.

For May 26, 1805 and June 7, 1805
Reprinted from The Journals of Lewis and Clark Expedition, volume 4, edited by Gary Moulton by permission of the University of Nebraska Press. Copyright © 1987 by the University of Nebraska Press.

For August 17, 1805
Reprinted from The Journals of Lewis and Clark Expedition, volume 5, edited by Gary Moulton by permission of the University of Nebraska Press. Copyright © 1987 by the University of Nebraska Press.

For November 7, 1805
Reprinted from The Journals of Lewis and Clark Expedition, volume 6, edited by Gary Moulton by permission of the University of Nebraska Press. Copyright © 1990 by the University of Nebraska Press.

Every reasonable effort has been made to properly acknowledge ownership of all material used. Any omissions or mistakes are not intentional and, if brought to the publisher's attention, will be corrected in future editions.

PHOTO AND ART CREDITS

Cover (detail) and Back Cover and Title Page (complete): Maynard Dixon, Wild Horses of Nevada, 1926. Oil on canvas, 44 x 50 inches. Collection of the William A. Karges Family Trust, courtesy William Karges Gallery, Los Angeles. Page 3: Walter Ufer, 1876-1936, Where the Desert Meets the Mountains. Oil on canvas, 36.5 x 40.5 inches. Photo by James O. Milmoe, courtesy of The Anschutz Collection. Pages 4-5: Edward S. Curtis, Cañon de Chelly, silver print, 1904. NAA, Smithsonian Institution, Washington, D.C. Page 9: T and MR, The Granger Collection; BL, George Caleb Bingham, 1811-1879, Fur Traders Descending the Missouri. The Metropolitan Museum of Art, Morris K. Jesup Fund, 1933. (33.61). Page 10: T, Robert Lindeux, Trail of Tears. Woolaroc Museum, Bartlesville, OK; B, Brown Brothers. Page 11: T, Brown Brothers; M, Solomon D. Butcher Collection, Nebraska State Historical Society. Page 17: (inset) The Granger Collection. Page 18: John Stevens, 1819-1879, Indian Massacre of 1862 (panel 17). Oil on canvas, 0126.2200. © Gilcrease Museum, Tulsa, OK. Page 31: Unknown Artist, Miss Denison, C. 1785. National Gallery of Art, from the Edgar William and Bernice Chrysler Garbisch Collection. Acc. #1980.62.28. Page 34: George Caleb Bingham, Daniel Boone Escorting Settlers through the Cumberland Gap, 1851-52. Oil on canvas 36.5 x 50.25 inches. Washington University Gallery of Art, St. Louis, Gift of Nathaniel Phillips, 1890. Page 38: William Clark, map, American Philosophical Society; William Clark, elkskin-bound journal, Missouri Historical Society. Page 40: BL, William Clark, Missouri Historical Society; BR, William Clark, American Philosophical Society. Page 41: William Clark, Missouri Historical Society. Pages 42 and 45: William Clark, American Philosophical Society. Page 47: Edward S. Curtis, The Scout-Apache, platinum print, C. 1906. NAA, Smithsonian Institution, Washington, D.C. Page 48: Whig Political Poster, photo by Richard Walker, New York State Historical Association, Cooperstown, NY Pages 50-51: Edward S. Curtis, The Rush Gatherer-Kutenai, orotone print, C. 1904. NAA, Smithsonian Institution, Washington, D.C.; (inset) Vash Gon-Jicarilla, platinum print, C. 1904. NAA, Smithsonian Institution, Washington, D.C. Pages 52 and 58: NAA, Smithsonian Institution, Washington, D.C. Page 62: Solomon D. Butcher Collection, Nebraska State Historical Society. Page 63: Breton Littlehales/National Geographic Society Image Collection. Pages 64 and 65: Nebraska State Historical Society. Page 66: T, Evelyn Cameron from Photographing Montana 1844-1928, The Life and Work of Evelyn Cameron by Donna M. Lucey. Alfred A. Knopf Publishers; ML, State Historical Society of North Dakota, #BO338; MR, The Kansas State Historical Society. Page 67: (inset) The Granger Collection; B, Kansas State Historical Society. Page 69: Harvey Dunn, The Homesteader's Wife, 1916. South Dakota Art Museum Collection. Page 82: N. C. Wyeth. Reprinted with permission. Page 89: Denver Public Library Western Collection. Photo by N. H. Rose. Page 90: (inset) © Bettmann/Corbis. Pages 90-91: State Historical Society of Colorado. Pages 92-93: The Granger Collection. Page 94: (inset) Brown Brothers. Pages 99-95: The Granger Collection. Page 98: Culver Pictures, Inc. Page 100: (inset) Seabright Collection. Pages 100-101 and 111: Culver Pictures, Inc. Page 113: Photonica. Page 115: Mark Chickinelli. Page 116: T, The Granger Collection; B, © John Bryson/Corbis-Sygma. Pages 124-125: Ferruccio Sardella. Pages 126 and 131: © Amos Nachoum/Corbis. Pages 128 and 129: © Norbert Wu/Peter Arnold, Inc. Pages 133 and 142: Vivienne Flesher.